For she who is my wife, who rather likes that last bit with Dodo in.

CONTENTS

OVERVIEW

Serial Title: *The Massacre* (aka *The Massacre of St Bartholomew's Eve*)

Writer: John Lucarotti ('War of God', 'The Sea Beggar', 'Priest of Death'), John Lucarotti and Donald Tosh ('Bell of Doom')

Director: Paddy Russell

Original UK Transmission Dates: 5 February 1966 – 26 February 1966

Running Time: 'War of God': 24m 51s

'The Sea Beggar': 24m 43s

'Priest of Death': 24m 33s

'Bell of Doom': 25m 6s

UK Viewing Figures: 'War of God': 8.0 million

'The Sea Beggar': 6.0 million

'Priest of Death': 5.9 million

'Bell of Doom': 5.8 million

Regular Cast: William Hartnell (Dr Who / The Abbot of Amboise), Peter Purves (Steven)

Guest Cast: Eric Thompson (Gaston), David Weston (Nicholas), John Tillinger (Simon), Edwin Finn (Landlord), Christopher Tranchell (Roger), Erik Chitty (Preslin), Annette Robertson (Anne Chaplet), Clive Cazes (Captain of the Guard), Reginald Jessup (Servant), André Morell (Marshal Tavannes), Leonard Sachs (Admiral de Coligny), Cynthia Etherington (Old Woman), Joan Young (Catherine de

Medici), Barry Justice (Charles IX), Michael Bilton (Teligny), Norman Claridge (Priest), Will Stampe (1st Man), Ernest Smith (2nd Man), John Slavid (Officer), Jack Tarran (1st Guard), Leslie Bates (2nd Guard), Jackie Lane (Dodo)

Antagonists: Catherine de Medici, the Abbot of Amboise

Novelisation: *Doctor Who: The Massacre* by John Lucarotti. **The Target Doctor Who Library** #122

Sequels and Prequels: 'Brief Encounter: The Meeting'

Responses:

'Whatever differences there may have been between Lucarotti and Tosh, their creative conflict gave birth to a story that is full of incident, atmosphere and fascinating period detail, with some rich and finely-drawn characters accorded some wonderful lines of dialogue.'

[David J Howe and Stephen James Walker, *The Television Companion*, p82]

SYNOPSIS

NB For a fuller treatment, see Chapter 2, 'What Happens in *The Massacre*?'

War of God

The Doctor takes advantage of his arrival in 16th-century Paris to seek the acquaintance of a scientific pioneer named **Preslin**. He finds him about to flee his pharmacy, fearing the persecution of free thinkers by the **Abbot of Amboise**.

Left behind in a pub, **Steven** befriends **Gaston**, a viscount in service of the prince **Henry of Navarre**, and **Nicholas**, the **Admiral de Coligny**'s secretary. Both men and their masters are affiliated with France's Protestant minority, the Huguenots, and are uneasy at the growing religious tension following Henry's marriage to the Catholic sister of **the King of France**.

The drinkers shelter **Anne Chaplet**, a Huguenot servant fleeing the employ of the Abbot of Amboise after she heard frightening hints of a conspiracy against Protestants. When **Colbert**, his secretary, tells him this, the Abbot is displeased. It is revealed that he looks exactly like the Doctor.

The Sea Beggar

The next day the Abbot arrives with his men to seek Anne, who has taken refuge with Steven at Admiral de Coligny's house. Steven is convinced that his friend is impersonating the cleric, but their connection causes Gaston to denounce Steven as a spy.

In an effort to resolve the confusion, Steven visits the Abbot's house to speak to him. Instead he overhears Colbert and **Tavannes**, the Marshall of France, discussing a plan to assassinate a target codenamed 'the Sea Beggar' – a nickname referring to the Dutch, whom de Coligny has been persuading the King to support in a naval campaign against the Spanish. Gaston's distrust of Steven prevents him from telling his Huguenot friends of his discovery, however.

Priest of Death

After a night spent at Preslin's abandoned pharmacy, Steven and Anne return to the Abbot's house. Through further eavesdropping, Steven learns the location and victim of the planned assassination. He informs Nicholas, but too late to prevent de Coligny from being shot on his way home from an acrimonious meeting with the King, Marshall Tavannes and **the Queen Mother**. The news of the attempt on de Coligny's life provokes an angry confrontation between the King and his mother, whom he correctly suspects of instigating the plot.

De Coligny is only wounded, however, and Tavannes orders the Abbot killed for his agent's failure. He has the cleric's body dumped in the street and the Huguenots blamed for his death, inciting an anti-Protestant riot.

Bell of Doom

The Queen Mother has convinced her son that the Protestants are a threat to his reign, and he has sealed an order for the deaths of all the Huguenots in Paris. However, Tavannes persuades the Queen Mother to avoid a war against the Protestant powers by allowing her son-in-law Henry of Navarre to escape.

Believing that the Doctor is dead, Steven and Anne ransack Preslin's pharmacy for the TARDIS key, but are interrupted by the arrival of the real Doctor. He is alarmed to learn of recent events, and even more when Anne tells him that the date is 23 August 1572, the eve of St Bartholomew's Day. He sends Anne away to hide, and insists that he and Steven leave Paris as the planned massacre begins.

Aboard the TARDIS, the Doctor tells Steven that they could never have altered the course of history, though it entailed the deaths of de Coligny and thousands of others. Steven accuses him of abandoning Anne to die with them, and resolves to leave the TARDIS at their next landing.

He does so, and the Doctor is left alone for an introspective moment – but is soon interrupted by **Dodo**, a young Londoner who has witnessed an accident on a common and mistakes the TARDIS for a police public call box. The Doctor hastily leaves, with Dodo and Steven aboard, to avoid discovery by the police. Dodo reveals that her full name is Dorothea Chaplet, and that her family were originally French. Steven chooses to take this as evidence that Anne survived the Massacre.

NOTES ON TERMINOLOGY

Characters from this serial who are historical figures have their names and titles rendered as per the scripts, even when these are abbreviations or elisions of names and titles (e.g. 'Marshall Tavannes', not Gaspard de Saulx, Knight of Tavannes, who among many other public offices held the title of Marshall of France).

French dynastic names using 'de', (e.g. 'Charles de Teligny') are in the absence of the forename or title, more properly rendered in English without the 'de', (e.g. it should be 'Teligny's army' not 'de Teligny's army'). The serial, however, consistently uses 'de Teligny' (etc.) as an Anglophone-style surname, and this style is adopted here for the serial's versions of these people. For historical persons relevant to the serial but who do not appear, English spellings and terms are generally preferred (e.g. 'Henry of Navarre', not Henri).

English spellings are also preferred for other French proper nouns, except when both are needed for direct comparison.

This volume adopts, in line with **Black Archive** house style, *The Massacre* as the overarching title of the four episodes of **Doctor Who** transmitted with the individual titles 'War of God', 'The Sea Beggar', 'Priest of Death' and 'Bell of Doom'. (For an extended discussion of this 'issue', please see Appendix 4, 'Title Fight'.)

In deference to this, while the serial is '*The Massacre*', the event with which it climaxes is 'the Massacre'. (See Appendix 3, 'A Note on Etymology'.)

Equally, the series' main character is consistently referred to as 'the Doctor' (not 'Doctor Who' or 'Dr Who') and his time machine is 'the TARDIS'; it both always takes the definitive article and is rendered in ALL CAPS. These conventions of editorial incidentals largely postdate the production of this serial.

All of these 'house rules' are suspended within direct quotations.

INTRODUCTION

For a hundred-minute television serial produced within living memory, *The Massacre* (1966) offers a complex set of interlocking challenges for anyone attempting anything beyond a surface engagement with it. It is, at time of writing anyway, perhaps the most conspicuously absent of **Doctor Who**'s notorious 'missing stories'. No copy of any episode is known to survive. There are no known extant clips and only a handful of photographs exist. There are not even any Tele-Snaps[1].

The scripts, fortunately, are available, safely archived at the BBC. There is also an audio recording of the serial, taped from a television using a microphone during the programmes' single UK transmission. The latter has been released on CD, with explanatory narration included where needed, and the former are included as a PDF on some later editions of the disc. This, objectively, makes it better represented than much 'missing' 1960s television. Yet The Massacre is something of a special case, with additional complications related to its drafting and authorship requiring our engagement and yet more inevitably arise from any interaction with the difficult historical topic with which the serial deals.

---

[1] Tele-Snaps was a now obsolete service offered to television professionals by John Cura, the sole owner and operator of the company that provided it, that is now invaluable to those researching television history. Cura used special equipment to photograph programming from a television screen during transmission, providing a permanent record of ephemeral broadcasts in the era before home video. Many 'missing' Doctor Who serials survive in Tele-Snap form.

The scripts for the serial share the writer's credit (unevenly, of which more later) between freelance author John Lucarotti and **Doctor Who**'s then Story Editor, Donald Tosh. (A series' Story Editor was, at this point in the corporation's history, a BBC member of staff responsible for commissioning scripts, working with writers and ensuring the results were producible. It was far from unknown for Story Editors to have to redraft freelancers' scripts themselves.)

Tosh has indicated that the impetus for a story set in Paris in August 1572, one of the bloodiest flashpoints of the decades-long series of conflicts usually known as the French Wars of Religion, came from Lucarotti[2], whereas Lucarotti recalled that the idea was Tosh's[3]. Both agree the idea arose after Tosh and his boss, producer John Wiles, had, on 24 June 1965, rejected a second draft of Lucarotti's storyline concerning the Viking, Erik the Red. This had been requested, if not formally commissioned, from Lucarotti by the production office under Wiles' predecessor, Verity Lambert.

Doctor Who stories set in human history almost always include some sort of alien threat to the historical period portrayed, but this was not always the case. During its first three years on air **Doctor Who**'s production teams divided, as a matter of policy, its stories roughly equally into two categories: 'future' – science fiction stories set on alien worlds, involving monsters or both – and 'past' – serials set in human history which, initially, had no science fiction elements except the presence of the series' leads in the historical

---

[2] Hearn, Marcus, 'Script Editing Who: Donald Tosh'. *Doctor Who Magazine* (DWM) #191.
[3] Russell, Gary, 'Off the Shelf'. DWM #124.

period[4]. These categories quickly broke down, with the 'future' 'Flight Through Eternity' (*The Chase* episode 3, 1965) placing the Daleks onto the deck of the *Mary Celeste* in 1872, but the boundaries were largely maintained until *The Highlanders* (1966-67), the last 'past' story as originally defined.

Lucarotti had written the two earliest, and most admired, 'past' **Doctor Who** serials and was initially keen to write a third[5].

Having been commissioned on 9 July 1965, Lucarotti delivered first drafts of all four episodes on the 20th of the same month. Second drafts were requested and these were received from Lucarotti across September and October 1965, with the fourth episode delivered on 8 October. (This turnaround may seem literally incredible, but it is not unknown in 1960s television; it may also be that Lucarotti began work before the formal commission was granted, which was also far from uncommon in the television practices of the time.)

It would be reasonable to assume that the process of creating the second drafts involved notes from Tosh, but these do not survive, and Tosh does not recall any detail concerning this.

---

[4] There was also a third internal category of 'sideways', but this was so rarely used that confidently ascribing it more than two serials, *The Edge of Destruction* and *Planet of Giants* (both 1964), is very difficult indeed.

[5] The second to fourth episodes of the first **Doctor Who** serial are set in the past, but not in recognisable human history. They are not, to attempt to make a distinction, 'period drama' or 'historical fiction'.

What Tosh **does** recall is that he was very unhappy with what he received from Lucarotti, and that he was forced to undertake extensive rewrites. These were, he later stated, largely required in order to correct serious historical inaccuracies contained within the scripts:

> 'John Lucarotti sent in a script, and he hadn't had any time to do his research, which was very unlike him. He had missed the whole point of the story, and everything else that was going in. It's a period I know quite a bit about, with the Massacre of Saint Bartholomew's Eve. I told John a lot of what he had written was rubbish, we had a huge great row, and I told Johnnie [Wiles], "We're going to have to commission a new story." But he said, "No, we've got to do it, that's what we've committed to," so I had to go away and rewrite it from page one.'[6]

> 'I took two days off, went to the reading room at the British Museum and literally saturated myself in all the historical detail, after which I just came back and wrote *The Massacre*.'[7]

Leaving issues of the historical authenticity of the serial to one side for a few thousand words, there is a potential practical consideration that may have contributed to Tosh's decision to undertake such a substantial rewrite. In its earliest years **Doctor Who** was recorded episodically, on a weekly schedule, and in most weeks of the year. It was rehearsed Monday to Friday and recorded

---

[6] Smith, Kenny, 'Doctor Who story editor Donald Tosh on his contribution to the Time Lord's series in 1965-66'.
[7] Stevens, Alan, 'Donald Tosh Interview'.

in an electronic videotape studio environment, in roughly narrative order, on a Friday evening. This means of production, a mix of the traditions of repertory theatre and radio, and eccentric to 21st-century eyes, dominated British television in the 1960s and would survive, increasingly modified, as the dominant form for much of the 20th century. (Indeed it remains a significant mode of production for situation comedy.)

This year-round schedule meant that members of the series' regular cast were, like salaried employees, entitled to weeks of holiday, and the weekly structure of that schedule meant that actors who took them would be absent for the episode made that week. For example, in the first series of **Doctor Who**, William Hartnell is wholly absent from 'The Screaming Jungle' and 'The Snows of Terror' (*The Keys of Marinus* episodes 3 and 4, 1964), while Jacqueline Hill is absent from 'A Race Against Death' and 'Kidnap' (*The Sensorites* episodes 4 and 5, 1964).

A way of ensuring a small appearance by an absent cast member in an early **Doctor Who** episode was to utilise some of the serial pre-filming allowance to shoot a brief scene featuring them ahead of the recording day. Most 1960s **Doctor Who** serials had budgeted a limited amount of location filming, or of film shooting within a non-electronic studio environment, in order to achieve scenes that could not be staged within a television studio dependent on mains electricity, e.g. scenes involving water or fire. (When added to the finished programme these 'Tele-Cines' were referred to by the abbreviation T/C to differentiate them from the videotaped material.) This would necessitate the cast member being absent for some of the rehearsals for an earlier episode in order to shoot the scene, which would normally be recorded midweek and a few weeks in hand. (Again, for example, in the first series of **Doctor Who**, William Russell appears in 'Guests of Madame Guillotine' and 'A Change of Identity' (*The Reign of Terror* episodes 2 and 3, 1964) only in pre-filmed material.)

'The Sea Beggar' is an example of the second kind of absence; William Hartnell is present only in a single (wordless) scene shot at Ealing in the first week of January 1966, the same week 'The Abandoned Planet' (*The Daleks' Master Plan* episode 11, 1966), was recorded.

It is possible, although there is no way to be certain as the relevant paperwork no longer exists, that part of the reason for the rewrite was to accommodate Hartnell's unavailability for the studio recording scheduled for 28 January 1966, and that his absence was not part of Lucarotti's brief. Hartnell, unlike his co-stars, was already contracted to appear in the **Doctor Who** episode made that week of 1966 when Lucarotti delivered his original draft of the second episode in July 1965, but that does not mean his absence **must** have been arranged that far in advance.

Indeed, the Doctor has a far greater role in the extant rehearsal scripts for the last two episodes of *The Daleks' Master Plan* (shot two and three weeks before 'The Sea Beggar' respectively) than he does in the camera scripts which were eventually shot, and which are represented on the surviving audio recordings. The Doctor only appears in the first quarter of 'The Abandoned Planet' and the final quarter of 'The Destruction of Time' (*The Daleks' Master Plan* episode 12, 1966). No one appears to know the reason for this change, but it does indicate that Hartnell's contributions to episodes made during this period were being amended and reduced at short notice, making it more than possible that this is indeed what happened with 'The Sea Beggar' and is in part the reason for it being rewritten.

Hartnell's absence, whether initially planned for or not, was especially challenging in the case of this serial. As the series' titular lead, Hartnell usually had a good deal of screen time in **Doctor Who**, but *The Massacre* had always been intended as a serial where Hartnell would get to demonstrate his versatility as an actor, by playing another character in addition to the Doctor. Hartnell wanted to play a villain in **Doctor Who**, and obviously didn't think that the sections of 'The Death of Doctor Who' and 'The Planet of Decision' (*The Chase* episodes 5 and 6, 1965) in which he also played the Daleks' evil robot duplicate of the Doctor fulfilled this desire. (His own preference was that he played the Doctor's villainous son(!)).

It was decided that this serial would be written around the conceit of Hartnell also playing a villainous character who would be noted as the Doctor's doppelganger within the fiction: the Abbot of Amboise. The Abbot was to be a Catholic churchman, committed to the persecution of members of other Christian denominations and deeply involved in a conspiracy against the life of one of the King's principal advisors, the Huguenot Admiral de Coligny.

Lucarotti always maintained that the idea behind the serial was that, as part of the action, the Doctor would be called upon to impersonate the Abbot[8], a plot movement that is almost always a feature of this kind of story and which would allow further

---

[8] Russell, 'Off The Shelf'.

demonstration of Hartnell's powers as an actor. This is the route adopted in the slightly later **Doctor Who** serial *The Enemy of the World* (1967), in which Patrick Troughton plays both the Doctor and his double, Leader Salamander. There the Doctor impersonates Salamander and indeed Salamander eventually impersonates the Doctor, leading to Troughton giving four distinct performances: the Doctor, Salamander, the Doctor pretending to be Salamander and Salamander pretending to be the Doctor.

The difficulty of such doubling within a 1960s videotape environment is another possible reason for the rewrite. In-sequence recording, even with pauses for costume changes, does not lend itself to one actor playing two parts easily, especially if they need to switch from one part to the other and then back again. In *The Enemy of the World*, made almost exactly two years later, Troughton principally plays one character in each episode (e.g. the Doctor appears in a single scene in episode 3) and some episodes were shot out of narrative order to facilitate his costume and makeup changes. When *The Massacre* was made, **Doctor Who**'s first experiment in recording an episode wholly out of order for practical reasons, 'The Bomb' (*The Ark* episode 4, 1966), was still a month away; it was a radical departure from production norms pushed for by the innovative director, Michael Imison. (Imison would, on the day of its recording, find that he had been 'let go' from his position as a BBC staff director, in part because the radicalism of his ideas about production did not fit in with those of his head of department, Gerald Savory.)

The nature of a videotaped studio recording also made it impossible for both characters played by a single actor to be seen onscreen together in videotaped scenes. *The Enemy of the World* only has one scene in which both the Doctor and Salamander appear, and that was pre-filmed at Ealing. Even then, they only appear in the same shot once. (There is also a scene in Episode 1 where the Doctor watches a pre-filmed insert of Salamander.)

As it stands, and we'll look at this in detail later, it seems certain that in the final scripts for *The Massacre*, in the version of the story that was made and transmitted and is available on CD, the Doctor does not impersonate the Abbot at all. Steven spends most of the serial believing he does, and the matter is left ambiguous to the audience for most of the serial, but is then resolved. Hartnell plays the Abbot only in 'The Sea Beggar' and 'Priest of Death' and the Doctor only in 'Bell of Doom'. He plays both parts (the Abbot for one shot and a single line of dialogue and without credit) in 'War of God'.

Whatever practical concerns may have pushed Tosh's rewrite, the results of it would cause immediate conflict between Lucarotti and the **Doctor Who** production office.

That Tosh made substantial revisions to all four episodes' scripts is something never disputed by Lucarotti[9], who later stated that the transmitted drafts were not simply more Tosh's work than his own but that Tosh had 'written them'[10] rather than merely amended them. On learning of the scale of Tosh's rewrites, Lucarotti asked for his name to be omitted from the programme's credits.

---

[9] Conversely, Tosh's similar claims to have written most of *The Daleks' Master Plan* after Terry Nation failed to deliver more than a few pages of material have failed to stand up to much scrutiny, partially because earlier drafts of those episodes **do** survive.
[10] Russell, 'Off The Shelf'.

Tosh has since indicated Lucarotti's request not to be credited was adhered to[11], although Lucarotti has said that he later rescinded his request on advice from his agent[12].With the serial unavailable and no Tele-Snaps extant it is impossible to wholly verify either statement. The camera scripts indicate an intention to credit, and that transparencies doing so were prepared. The Programme as Broadcast form, a BBC internal document which exists for every programme and contains a list of credited and uncredited contributors, also contains writing credits. The first three episodes are credited to Lucarotti alone and the fourth is ascribed to Lucarotti and Tosh. This does not mean, however, that Tosh only contributed to the writing of the fourth instalment. As BBC staff, Tosh could receive no authorship credit for the first three episodes regardless of the level of his contribution; with BBC policy holding that any rewriting of freelancers' scripts by a Story Editor was covered by the Story Editor credit they received in the programme's closing titles.

However, Tosh was in the process of moving on from **Doctor Who** and his successor Gerry Davis officially beginning work with, and was the credited Story Editor on, 'Bell of Doom'. This meant that Tosh, now officially freelance with regards to **Doctor Who**, could receive a co-authorship credit. (He was, however, not assigned any copyright in the episode.) It is, it must be noted, certainly not wholly without precedent for a PasB form to not exactly match the onscreen credits of the transmitted programme to which it refers.

---

[11] Hearn, 'Script Editing Who, Donald Tosh'.
[12] Russell, 'Off The Shelf'.

Lucarotti himself considered Tosh to be the author of the final serial, while Tosh himself more usually refers to his version of the story as 'revised'[13] rather than written from scratch, (although see above) and estimates that the process took him 'about two weeks'. The scripts do bear signs of being written very quickly, e.g. in 'Bell of Doom', where Steven's reasons for returning to the TARDIS and the Doctor's for taking off with Dodo aboard are not so much opaque as wholly inchoate, and where the stage directions at one point refer to Dodo as 'Anne'. No copies of Lucarotti's rejected scripts are known to exist. Thus, while it is easy to establish that the version shot was ultimately Tosh's responsibility, it is much harder to ascertain how much, if any, of Lucarotti's drafts survived into the scripts that were recorded.

In the 1980s, Lucarotti was contacted by WH Allen's Target Books imprint. Target had produced novelisations - children's novellas based on **Doctor Who** television serials - very successfully since 1973. By the 1980s, the publisher was actively attempting to create a complete library of **Doctor Who** adaptations in such a form, and was seeking out people who had not worked on the series for 20 years and asking them to adapt their own screenplays. Lucarotti signed a contract to adapt all three of his serials, and produced well-reviewed books of *The Aztecs* (1964) and *Marco Polo* (1964). Then this happened:

> 'When I had finished the novels of the other two, I picked up these [*The Massacre*] scripts – I'd been hiding from them! – and I read them. Anyway, I thought, "Oh no, this isn't on. Never!" So I contacted WH Allen and said that I

---

[13] Hearn, 'Script Editing Who, Donald Tosh'.

thought it best to forget it, "I'll do the other two and we'll call it quits," and they were very nice and explained that all three were considered classics from the past, and to go on, do *The Massacre*.'[14]

The novella that Lucarotti subsequently wrote[15] is not based on his own original scripts, as they were before Tosh's rewrites, because they were already unavailable by the 1980s. Nor is it a retelling of the extant camera scripts which were supplied to him. The book is instead essentially a new work set in the same historical period, using (mostly) the same characters and the same premise, taking into account extra research Lucarotti did during the 1980s and incorporating some (small) sections of the final production scripts that may themselves be surviving pieces of Lucarotti's own lost 1965 version. It is also a version of the serial's narrative in which the Doctor's impersonation of the Abbot is key to almost all plot movements.

This essay discusses the serial and the novelisation as separate works, the latter in part derived from the former. However, due to the specific circumstances of the writing of both, the book is relevant to questions about the serial's authorship and the process of its composition in a way that is rare for a Target retelling. Therefore, we'll later look at how elements of the novelisation may represent Lucarotti's intentions for the rewritten original scripts. When interviewed Lucarotti did indicate the book 'incorporates the basic idea of the script'[16] he originally wrote, but equally, he freely

---

[14] Russell, 'Off The Shelf'.

[15] Lucarotti, John, *Doctor Who: The Massacre*.

[16] Russell, 'Off The Shelf'.

admitted that there are elements of the novelisation that were explicitly only formulated two decades after the serial's transmission.

CHAPTER 1: ADVENTURES IN HISTORY

Doctor Who is, in part, a time travel series and was devised with an educational bent in mind. Yet, within it, history is essentially used as a backdrop to adventure stories. The people of the past are people of the time of the serial's creation but in more complicated clothes. Exactly none of the substantive issues of the Jacobite uprising of 1745-46 are touched upon in *The Highlanders*, or any of the other dozens of episodes in which an actual Jacobite rebel appears. (It is occasionally passingly portrayed, quite inaccurately, as a war between Scotland and England.) *The Mark of the Rani* (1985) does not, despite featuring Sir Thomas Henry Liddell as a major character, engage with his opposition, when in parliament, to the Duke of Portland's government's attempts at Catholic relief. There are many other examples. (The serial, set in 1813, also pre-emptively raises him to the peerage as Baron Ravensworth, but this didn't happen until 1820.)

The Massacre, however, is not something which is set in a picture-book past utilising the names of people who actually lived as its characters. This is the **Doctor Who** serial which attempts to be the most responsive and responsible to the historical record; the one that takes most seriously its nature as a piece of drama set during real events and portraying people who actually lived. It tries to engage, within the limited confines of popular family drama, with the concerns of the events it portrays and with the characters as people of their time.

The Massacre has 15 named speaking characters. Of those, seven are demonstrably real people (and mostly people of sufficient note in their own lives as to be conspicuously embedded in the historical record) and two have a basis in history but are not (necessarily) real individuals[17]. Six are clearly fictional. Of those six, three are the Doctor, Steven Taylor and Dodo Chaplet, the last of whom only appears in the last five minutes of the final episode and not, in any case, in 16th-century France at all.

King Charles IX (1550-74), his mother Queen Catherine de Medici (1519-89), Admiral de Coligny (1519-72), and Marshall Tavannes (1509-75) are significant enough figures in 16th-century French history for anything other than asserting their reality to be redundant.

---

[17] To put this into context, only five real people have speaking roles in all of 1980s **Doctor Who**, and none at all in 1970s **Doctor Who**. Elsewhere in 1960s **Doctor Who**, there are two real people in *Marco Polo*, three in *The Reign of Terror*, four in *The Romans* (1965), six in *The Crusade* (1965), six in *The Chase*, one (possibly) in *The Myth Makers* (1965) (although this serial is something of a special case), two in *The Daleks' Master Plan* (1965-66), nine in *The Gunfighters* (1966) and two (both dubious) in *The Highlanders*. 21st-century **Doctor Who** offers us six in *The Shakespeare Code* (2007), three in *The Fires of Pompeii* (2008) and *The Pandorica Opens* (2010), two in *The Girl in The Fireplace* (2006) and *The Wedding of River Song* (2010) and one each in *The Unquiet Dead* (2005), *Tooth and Claw* (2006), *Voyage of the Damned* (2007), *The Unicorn and the Wasp* (2008), *The Beast Below* (2010), *Victory of the Daleks* (2010), *Vincent and the Doctor* (2010), *The Impossible Astronaut / Day of The Moon (2011), The Curse of the Black Spot* (2011), *Let's Kill Hitler* (2011), *Dinosaurs on a Spaceship* (2012) and *The Day of the Doctor* (2013). (This excludes cameos in which people play themselves, stock footage, uncredited extras and the appearance of (doubly) fictional versions of real people in the Land of Fiction in *The Mind Robber* (1968).)

Nicholas Muss (sometimes 'de la Moche') was a member of Coligny's staff. As in the serial, he was a German, but he was an interpreter who assisted in his master's diplomatic work, not Coligny's secretary. He died within minutes of the Admiral on the night of 23 August, killed by guards from the Cardinal of Lorraine's household as they stormed the Admiral's house to finish him off.

Charles de Teligny, who appears in 'Priest of Death' and 'Bell of Doom', was the Admiral's son-in-law. He too died in the Massacre, stabbed in a corridor at the Louvre by the palace guard on the 23rd and then bleeding to death while attempting to reach safety.

Lucarotti has indicated that Gaston is not a historical figure[18], but this is incorrect. The PasB credits him only as 'Gaston', but dialogue declares him the 'Viscount de Lérans'[19]. French catalogues of the births of the aristocracy give us a 'Gaston de Levis' (b1547), the son of 'Germain de Levis, Viscount de Lérans'[20]. This could be a coincidence, except that contemporary reports[21] indicate Gaston's

---

[18] Russell, 'Off The Shelf'.

[19] 'War of God', 'The Sea Beggar'.

[20] Aubert de la Chesnaye-Desbois, Francois Alexander Badier, *Dictionnaire de la Noblesse.*

[21] These include the posthumously published memoirs of Pierre de Bourdeille (1540-1614), usually referred to as 'Brantome'. While genuine, these are often regarded as partial and unreliable, despite Brantome's certain presence at many of the events he describes and contact with people on whom he opines, due to their unjudgementally frank sexual content. Brantome fought, at various times, on both sides during the French Wars of Religion.

presence in Paris in August 1572[22] as part of Henry of Navarre's party, and later – using the variant spelling 'Viscount de Leyrau' – his serious injury and narrow escape from death on the night of the 23rd after seeking the protection of Henry's bride. (That the serial's Gaston survived August 1572 is indicated by the story not showing a pre-filmed close-up of his corpse along with those of the other prominent Huguenots from the serial during the finale of 'Bell of Doom'. Incidentally, the Canadian city of Levis is named for a later Viscount of Laurens, a successor of Gaston's, and the House of Levis still exists.) This indicates that either Lucarotti researched the historic Gaston in 1965 and then forgot him when he came to write the book, or that Lerans' inclusion happened during Tosh's rewrites. Given that the main historical source for the lives of Muss and Gaston, both of whom are relatively obscure, is the same single book of documents, the former is more probable.

There was one man named Simon Duval(l) (b1546 or 1547) in Paris in 1572, but he was a (Catholic) shoemaker, not an aide to the Marshall of France. However, on Wednesday 20 August 1572 he was one of several people issued a licence to marry over the St Bartholomew's Day weekend coinciding with the Royal Wedding feast[23]. If **this** is a coincidence, it is a striking one, and it may be that Lucarotti (or Tosh) took the real man's name from a historical list in order to give it to his fictional counterpart. (The historical Duval(l) lived until at least 1580, when he is listed as the witness to another marriage.)

---

[22] Browning, William Shergold, *The History of the Huguenots During the Sixteenth century*, p88; D'Aubigne, Jean-Henri Merle, *Histoire de la Reformation au XVIie Siècle*, Vol II p19.

[23] 'Minutes. 1572, janvier – 1572, 27 août', Archives Nationales.

Another genuine historical figure, played by an extra who does not speak at all, never mind to any of the other characters, is the Admiral's would-be-assassin. Colbert lets slips that this man, called 'Bondot' in most conversations in the story is really called 'Maurevert'[24]. Charles de Louviers, Lord of Maurevert (1505-1583), who did use the codename Bondot[25], is universally identified as the most likely trigger-man in the events of 22 August 1572. (It is, incidentally, 'Bondot', not 'Bondeaux', in the script and the sources. Use of the latter, pseudo-French, spelling is hypercorrection.) The serial also equips Bondot, correctly, with an arquebus with which to shoot the Admiral.

The apothecary Charles Preslin, presented by the serial as a notable historical scientific pioneer, is a fiction. Roger Colbert too, has no counterpart in the historical Paris of 1572. Anne Chaplet is a fictional character.

This brings us to the question of the Abbot of Amboise. Amboise is a real town in France, these days perhaps most widely recognised as the place where Leonardo da Vinci died. It has been noted[26] that Amboise was the site of significant events in the French Wars of Religion, and that the Abbot may have been named for any of them, but that there was no Abbey there.

The former point is well made. The terms 'Amboise conspiracy' and 'Tumult of Amboise' are still attached to actions taken by the Huguenot Louis of Condé against Queen Catherine de Medici, her

[24] 'The Sea Beggar'.
[25] Bourgeon, Jean-Louis, *L'Assassinat de Coligny*, pp41, 56.
[26] Wood, Tat and Lawrence Miles, *About Time: The Unauthorized Guide to Doctor Who: 1963-1966 – Seasons 1 to 3*, p234.

son King Francis II (the older brother of the King of this serial) and the Guise family in 1560, and the original treaty conceding freedom of worship to Huguenots of 1563 was the Edict of Amboise.

The latter point, however, is not quite correct. There was in 1572 no 'Abbey of Amboise'. However, ten miles along the river from Amboise town there was the 11th-century abbey of Marmoutier. This Abbey was within the commune of Amboise and served the district. ('Commune' in this context is not a Marxist term, but a mediaeval level of administration of the French countryside partially derived from parish structures. They still operate, in a revised form, as of 2015. There is no exact equivalent in the United Kingdom.) Marmoutier Abbey in Amboise was founded by Saint Martin, the first in its long line of prominent Father Abbots. (It may also be significant, given the duality that is endlessly reiterated in this serial, that relics of Saint Martin, including sacramental oils, from this Abbey were used when Henry IV – the **Protestant** Henry of Navarre of this serial – was crowned and consecrated as a **Catholic** King of France in 1594.)

Philip Huraults (d.1539) was the last independent Abbot of Marmoutier, in that he both drew the living of the house and had responsibility for the monks within the institution. After this the Abbey came under the regime of Abbots in Commendation. (This was a convention whereby one person, not necessarily a churchman, took the title of Abbot and the income from the institution, while another, almost certainly a monk within the institution, was responsible for the day-to-day administration of the Abbey and good order of its monks, but without being named its Abbot.) Because of this, ascertaining exactly who the Abbot at Marmoutier Amboise was in 1572 is difficult, as the function was divided between at least two people, and the term is inconsistently applied after 1539. (For most of the first half of the 17th century the Abbot in Commendation was Cardinal Richelieu (1585-1642), who never set foot in the Abbey, but who does provide one of this serial's many small links with the work of the elder Alexander Dumas.)

More important though, for the purposes of our **Doctor Who** story at least, is the fact that, shortly after the Abbey was sacked by a Huguenot mob in 1562, a man called Chastillon travelled the local area proclaiming himself, wholly falsely, to be the Abbot of Marmoutier at Amboise[27], issuing edicts and encouraging his followers to occupy the site of the damaged Abbey. He caused considerable confusion for municipal authorities about his identity, and prompted a series of riots and public displays of disobedience, before being arrested and executed.

There really was a fake Abbot of Amboise during the French Wars of Religion.

It seems hugely implausible that this verifiable historical anecdote's convergence with elements of Lucarotti's storyline is coincidental: it is surely the inspiration for the Doctor impersonating the Abbot, and essentially the point of the entire story.

This story element's source in historical fact may also explain why the writer was so unhappy with the transmitted version of the

---

[27] Nelson, Eric, 'The Legacy of Iconoclasm: Religious war and the relic landscape of Tours, Blois and Vendôme, 1550-1750', *St Andrews Studies in French History and Culture* #6; Martène, Edmond, *Histoire de l'abbaye de Marmoutier* Volume 2, p376.

serial, in which the Doctor does not impersonate the Abbot, merely resembles him (see Chapter 2, 'What Happens In *The Massacre*?'), and his determination to restore it when novelising the serial two decades later.

The Massacre has more real people in, both proportionally and absolutely, than almost any other **Doctor Who** story, but none of them talk to the series' title character and only two of them are ever in the same scene, or even on the same set, as him. Steven Taylor converses extensively with Gaston and Nicholas, and is briefly (and unknowingly) in line of sight of Marshall Tavannes twice, but he does not talk to, or even meet with, the serial's more prominent historical personages, even the Admiral de Coligny (in whose house he lodges between the first two episodes).

Comments made by John Wiles in 1983 suggest that this is a result of deliberate action by the **Doctor Who** production office:

> 'We were fairly keen to find our way around this whole business of doing historical stories. Should the Doctor actually get involved with the main characters? Should he meet Catherine de Medici, or should he just get involved with peripheral events?'[28]

Decades later his Story Editor would echo these comments, saying:

> 'The fact is, there's not much point in doing a historical drama if you're going to get all the details wrong, but equally the more that is known about a certain period of

---

[28] Bentham, J Jeremy, 'John Wiles Interview', *Doctor Who Winter Special* 1983.

history, the more restrictive it becomes on your regular characters.'[29]

The second clause of this sentence cast some light on the unusual plotting of the story, wherein the significant historical figures are almost hermetically sealed away from the characters from the science fiction series in which they have found themselves. It may be a reflection of the almost puritan (and arguably impossible to sustain) attitude to presenting historical figures in the context of tea-time drama expressed separately by both Tosh and Wiles.

This then, is a serial with both a complex and difficult history and a complex relationship with difficult history. These are both topics that are worth discussing in detail. First, however, we need to achieve clarity about what happens in the story, when it happens and how it happens. This is necessary due to the scripts' use of a doppelganger of the series' main character who is also played by its star, and the ambiguous and sometimes opaque way the serial is plotted in order to facilitate this plot element. Additionally, there are story elements that were introduced (or possibly **re**introduced) for Lucarotti's prose adaptation which are sometimes assumed, in discussions of *The Massacre*, to be part of the transmitted serial when they're not, creating further opportunities for confusion.

---

[29] Stevens, 'Donald Tosh Interview'.

CHAPTER 2: WHAT HAPPENS IN THE MASSACRE?[30]

Each episode of *The Massacre* takes place across a different day, with 'The Sea Beggar', 'Priest of Death' and 'Bell of Doom' all beginning, in narrative terms, several hours after the previous episode concludes. As a consequence of this structure, no episode of the story, uniquely for episodic 20th-century television Doctor Who, begins with a reprise of the final scene of the previous episode in transmission order. The production team of John Wiles and Donald Tosh seem to have made a deliberate attempt to rid themselves of this convention during their brief tenure. Two episodes of *The Myth Makers* clearly lack a reprise from the previous instalment and pick up 'some time later'. Several episodes of *The Daleks' Master Plan* also lack direct reprises, and the final episode of *The Gunfighters*, another Wiles/Tosh commission, also has no reprise. Given the ubiquity of the cliff-hanger reprise in 20th-century **Doctor Who** it is likely this sudden rush of absences constitutes a (quickly reversed) change of policy.

War of God

20 August 1572

The Doctor and Steven arrive in 16th-century Paris, but are unaware of the exact day and date. The Doctor resolves to go and

---

[30] Apologies are made to the shade of John Dover Wilson.

meet Charles Preslin, an apothecary undertaking interesting work in the period, and drops Steven off for an afternoon in the pub on the way. In this tavern, they observe an argument developing between Simon Duval, a Catholic, and a group of young Huguenots led by Gaston, Viscount Lerans and the German Nicholas Muss, but do not become involved.

As the Doctor leaves this tavern, he is seemingly recognised and followed by a man. Steven makes to go after him, but is stopped by the landlord of the tavern, as he has not paid for his drink. Steven falls in with the Huguenots, who help him when the landlord attempts to short-change him. The Doctor meets Preslin at his shop. Preslin tells the Doctor that he and his professional colleagues are being persecuted a clergyman, the Abbot of Amboise.

A servant girl, Anne Chaplet, is pursued from a house that is being readied for the Abbot's use by guards from the Household of the Cardinal of Lorraine. Protected from the guards by Steven, Nicholas and Gaston, Anne reveals that she too is a Huguenot, and that she fled in terror after overhearing a conversation that mentioned the town of Vassy and the possibility that what happened there would happen 'again before the week was out'. It is explained to Steven that ten years before a large number of Huguenots were murdered in Vassy, simply because of their religion. Anne is a survivor of those events.

The end of the episode sees the Doctor already having set off alone on an ambiguous errand, after having discussed going to see the Abbot, but without either the Doctor or Preslin confirming (or denying) to the audience that this is what he's done. The Doctor's failure to return before Paris' curfew means Steven has to take up *an offer from Nicholas Muss to stay in the house of the Admiral de Coligny overnight. In the episode's final scene, the audience sees a man addressed as 'Father Abbot' in the company of Simon Duval and the man whom Steven believed followed the Doctor out of the tavern earlier. He is played by William Hartnell.*

It is clear from this episode that the Abbot is a real person who exists in the France of 1572. Preslin and Gaston are aware of him, and the staff at the Cardinal of Lorraine's Paris house are preparing for his arrival before the Doctor comes to Paris. Preslin has strong opinions on the Abbot's 'notorious' character and has direct personal experience of his persecution of apothecaries. However, this episode does not yet introduce the idea that the Abbot looks like the Doctor. It simply shows a man Colbert and Duval believe to be the Abbot, who is played by William Hartnell. No dialogue has, as yet, indicated that the Abbot and the Doctor resemble each other. Indeed the idea is distinctly absent from the scene in which the Doctor and Preslin discuss the Abbot. When taking this episode with the succeeding ones we have to assume that Preslin does not know the Abbot by sight, despite their history, otherwise he would never have let the Doctor into the shop. It may be relevant that in Lucarotti's novelisation (pp40-45, 55), Preslin and his fellow apothecaries recognise the Doctor as a notable Catholic immediately and shortly afterwards decide he is the Abbot.

It is possible **based on this episode alone** that the man seen in the final shot is not the Abbot, but the Doctor pretending to be him, without there being a physical resemblance between the Abbot and the Doctor.

We have already noted that Roger Colbert, the Abbot's 'temporal secretary', seems to have no historical counterpart. (Although Colbert is a common surname in Lorraine, the part of France which is the base of the Abbot's power and the name is, as such, a well-chosen one. There is also a character called Colbert in the earlier Paris-set **Doctor Who** serial *The Reign of Terror*.) This is not the only oddity concerning the character within 'War of God'. Colbert is, according to the camera script's stage directions and dialogue given to Steven in 'The Sea Beggar', the person who bumps into the Doctor as the latter leaves the tavern, appears to recognise him and then, without speaking, seems to follow him. The next time we see Roger he is in the company of the Abbot, and within the structure of the episode he must return to the Abbot's house more or less immediately, otherwise he would not be there to have the conversation that terrifies Anne three scenes later.

Colbert is reduced to a barely speaking part in Lucarotti's prose adaptation, and what remains of his plot function is absorbed by Simon Duvall. There he is described as 'a fat little man', adjectives which hardly describe actor Christopher Tranchell. Given that Lucarotti has a wholly different conception of the character (something untrue of any other named part shared by the serial and book), and considering the structural oddities within the story that follow the character, it is possible Colbert was either introduced into the story by Tosh, or was a smaller character whose role was expanded to fill a void created when the Doctor/Abbot was, as suggested above, more or less totally removed from the serial's middle half.

The Sea Beggar

21 August 1572

Having stayed at de Coligny's house overnight, Steven returns to the tavern to try and find the Doctor. With no sign of him, Steven returns to the Admiral's house, where Nicholas offers to help him. Nicholas and Gaston are visited by Colbert, who demands the return of Anne to the Abbot's service. They refuse. Gaston even goes to so far as to claim, when Anne is in the room, that she is a different woman entirely, a longstanding employee of the Admiral's called Genevieve. As Colbert leaves, he is seen through the window talking to a man that Steven recognises as the Doctor, but who Gaston and Nicholas recognise as the Abbot.

In parallel to this, we see Simon Duval discussing the Abbot's hunt for Anne with Marshall Tavannes. Tavannes does not trust the Abbot, and asks Duval to spy on him. Tavannes also becomes suspicious that there is an Englishman staying at the Admiral's house, thinking he may be a spy for (the Protestant) Queen Elizabeth's government. We also meet de Coligny for the first time, and are introduced to his enthusiasm for aiding 'the Dutch' in their war against Spain.

Steven and Nicholas look for the Doctor by travelling to Preslin's shop. It is empty and his neighbours state that Preslin was arrested for heresy two years before and has not been seen since. They sincerely wish him dead. This makes Nicholas more suspicious of Steven than before. Steven comes to the conclusion that the Doctor is impersonating the Abbot and when Nicholas refuses to let Steven go and look for him, Steven runs away from him. Steven makes his way to the Abbot's house where he eavesdrops through a window and hears Marshall Tavannes announce to Colbert and Duval that 'The Sea Beggar dies tomorrow'.

Steven returns to the Admiral's house, and in the absence of both Nicholas and Gaston, begins to look through papers. Gaston returns, discovering him, and is enraged. He considers killing Steven, but instead spares him and throws him out of the house. Steven wanders the streets aimlessly, eventually resolving to return to the Admiral's house, but instead bumps into Anne who has also left the Admiral's. Together they head to Preslin's shop. At the Admiral's house, the Admiral tells Nicholas that he believes he has succeeded in persuading the King to declare war on Spain and that the King has dubbed him 'the Sea Beggar' in recognition of this.

In relation to the plotting of this episode, it is worth emphasising that both Gaston and Nicholas correctly recognise the Abbot through the window **in the exact same moment** in which Steven mistakes him for the Doctor. There are several things that are odd about this.

Firstly, Gaston and Nicholas were in the tavern at the same time as the Doctor in the previous episode, and Nicholas saw him clearly enough to refer to him as 'the old man' when talking to Steven after his departure, but not clearly enough to decide he looked like the Abbot. (It is reasonable to assume this contrivance is part of the reason why, according to the few onset photographs that exist, that the Doctor wears a hat with a brim that casts a shadow over his face in 'War of God'. He does not wear this exact costume in any other serial or indeed any other episode of this serial.) Despite this, Nicholas is capable of being absolutely certain that a man in ecclesiastical dress that he sees for a few seconds is the Abbot, even though Steven, who knows the Doctor far better than Nicholas and Gaston know the Abbot, mistakes him for the Doctor in exactly the same amount of time. (The telecine, which is Hartnell's sole contribution to the episode, lasts for 18 seconds. The shots in the script suggest that Hartnell's face would not be clearly visible for all of these 18 seconds.) In that moment in which Steven, Gaston and Nicholas see the Abbot, he is in the company of Roger Colbert, whom Steven has just identified to the audience as being the man the Doctor bumped into while leaving the tavern last week. (This whole sequence forms an odd accompaniment to the manner in which, in the first scene of this episode, Gaston and Nicholas recognise Roger on sight and even know his job title, and yet they did not notice him enter the tavern last week.)

If the first two episodes are taken together, with no knowledge of what follows, the implication is that Colbert misidentified the Doctor as the Abbot upon seeing him in the tavern, and that is why he followed him away from it. This scene gives the audience, and Steven, strong reasons to believe that the man outside is indeed the Doctor, not the real Abbot, but also introduces the plot element of the physical resemblance between the two men, which has not been mentioned before this scene. (However, the Doctor cannot have been with Colbert and impersonating the Abbot since then, because he visits Preslin later in 'War of God', and when he does so has no knowledge of the Abbot's existence.)

This plot point is returned to, and given more substance, in the sixth scene of 'The Sea Beggar', where Colbert has this conversation with Duval.

41

DUVAL

Oh, very well. Tell me what you know about the Abbot.

COLBERT

He's been specially appointed by the Cardinal.

DUVAL

I don't mean that. How long have you known him?

COLBERT

I only met him yesterday, but he's worked for His Eminence the Cardinal of Lorraine for many years and has done him many services.

DUVAL

You saw him for the first time yesterday?

COLBERT

No, I met him for the first time. I saw him once at an encyclical meeting held by the Cardinal.

DUVAL

And that was the only time you've seen him?

COLBERT

Yes.

This strongly suggests to the audience, **particularly** if they can recall the near-collision between Colbert and the Doctor, that Steven is correct and the Doctor is impersonating the Abbot. It provides Colbert with a **reason** to recognise the Doctor as the (newly arrived) Abbot, to go with the **opportunity** 'War of God' has already given him.

At this point then, the serial itself is pointing quite strongly to the man seen outside the window being the Doctor engaged in an impersonation of the Abbot, and this is what Steven, who is the audience's identification figure and the only speaking character in the episode they have any familiarity with, fervently believes. (Steven's notion that the Doctor is impersonating the Abbot is not inherently ridiculous. The Doctor is prone to both disguising himself[31] and taking advantage of occasions of mistaken identity[32].)

Tosh has described this plot motion thus:

> 'At one point Steven sees the Abbot and naturally mistakes him for the Doctor. Neither he nor the viewer is entirely sure whether the Doctor is impersonating the Abbot or whether they are actually two different people.'[33]

Colbert, who features strongly in this episode, is effectively the Abbot's assistant and as such forms a mirror to Steven, who is the Doctor's. (He is also, continuing the mirroring, the Abbot's secretary, just as Lerans and Muss are secretaries to Navarre and the Admiral respectively, although their historical counterparts were not.) The two men separately spend 'The Sea Beggar' hunting for the Abbot. Steven does so because he believes him to be the

---

[31] E.g. as Zephon in *Day of Armageddon* (*The Daleks' Master Plan* episode 2, 1965).

[32] E.g. when he is assumed to be Zeus in *Temple of Secrets* (*The Myth Makers* episode 1).

[33] Hearn, 'Script Editing Who, Donald Tosh'.

Doctor, and Colbert because he knows him to be the Abbot. Meanwhile, the Abbot engages in a heavy-handed off-screen search for Anne Chaplet because he fears she will betray their plans concerning the Sea Beggar; but it is Steven, not the Abbot or his men, who finds Anne, quite by accident, as the episode draws to a close.

The idea of mistaken identity, with resulting dualism, is encountered elsewhere in 'The Sea Beggar'. Early in the episode, Anne enters the room when Gaston is talking to Colbert, and Colbert recognises her. Gaston engages in a wholly unconvincing deception over Anne's identity, claiming she is a servant of longstanding in the Admiral's household. Colbert nevertheless finds it impossible to refute this paper-thin deception and has to leave. This forms a counterpoint to the main Doctor-Abbot ambiguity, of which it forms a microcosm, but without the visuals it is impossible to tell how the ambiguity of this scene is played out onscreen. If this seems a stretch, then it worth considering deleted material from earlier in the episode which would made this moment less ambiguous if retained.

The material below is present in the camera script for Scene 3, but not in the transmitted episode.

> ANNE COMES IN WITH A TRAY ON WHICH THERE IS A JUG OF WINE AND TWO GLASSES.
>
> SHE IS LET IN BY ANOTHER SERVANT WHO CROSSES TO NICHOLAS AND WHISPERS SOMFTHING TO HIM.
>
> ANNE PUTS DOWN THE TRAY.

GASTON

Girl! Come here.

ANNE LOOKS NERVOUSLY AT HIM.

SHE DOESN'T SPEAK.

GASTON

What exactly did you hear at the Abbot's house?

ANNE

Like I said, Monsieur, the Captain spoke of Vassy and then that something would happen before the end of the week.

GASTON

Have you remembered nothing else?

ANNE

No, Monsieur. That was all I heard then I ran away.

THE SERVANT LEAVES CLOSING THE DOOR BEHIND HIM.

NICHOLAS TURNS TO GASTON.

NICHOLAS

Leave the girl alone.

GASTON

Did the word Vassy and the phrase follow one another?

ANNE

I don't know what you mean.

NICHOLAS

She can't tell us any more. You're frightening her. All right, Anne. You can go.

GASTON

Look - all I'm trying to do...

ANNE BOBS A SORT OF CURTSY AT NICHOLAS, SCUTTLES TOWARDS THE DOOR.

JUST AS SHE GETS THERE A SERVANT SHOWS STEVEN IN.

The removal of this moment means that when Anne enters the room during Colbert's argument with Gaston, the audience has not seen her for a week. As she does not speak, the viewer (and even more so the listener, the only audience the serial has in posterity) cannot be wholly certain that it is Anne at all.

In their scene at the Louvre, Tavannes calls de Coligny a man who 'see shadows where there is no sun'. He is being disingenuous, in that not only is there a plot but he, Tavannes, is a part of it, but he also seems to be alluding to 'On Monsieur's Departure', a poem by the English Queen Elizabeth. This in part reads:

> My care is like my shadow in the sun
> Follows me flying, flies when I pursue it.

This might sound implausible, but the lyric is one of the best known of its decade and was composed about Hercule Francois, a younger brother of the King of France seen in the serial. Elizabeth herself is mentioned several times in the serial, including here. It is more or less impossible to research Elizabeth I's relations with France – something which is in part the subject of this scene – without coming across the lyric.

The episode is a series of unresolved quests – or a series of scenes which consist of little more than atmospheric wheel-spinning. Steven leaves the Admiral's house and goes to the tavern, then back to the Admiral's house. Then to Preslin's shop. Then to the Abbot's. Then back to the Admiral's. Then wanders the streets. Then heads back to the Admiral's, but meets Anne instead along the way and together they return to Preslin's shop. All Steven has accomplished is to learn that 'The Sea Beggar dies tonight', a phrase that does not make sense to him and, based on what the audience has been told, implies some sort of threat to the oft-mentioned but never seen Dutch.

The cliff-hanger for this episode, which reveals that the title of the episode is Tavannes' codename for de Coligny, is unusual for **Doctor Who** in that it is not an incident or a direct, immediate threat, but a plot revelation and a long-term threat to someone we have only just met, who has not met either of the series' leads and who is not even driving the story in their own right.

Priest of Death

22 August 1572

In Preslin's shop, Anne inadvertently wakes Steven and they exchange a few bad-tempered words, before Steven decides to go back to the Abbot's house, to try and learn more about whatever is being plotted.

At the Louvre, Admiral de Coligny, Charles de Teligny and Marshall Tavannes compete for the attention and favour of King Charles IX. De Coligny repeats his desire to see France go to war with Spain in order to aid the Dutch. Tavannes insists that France cannot afford a war, the coffers being empty after decades of civil disturbances. Possible sources of funding and aid, such as leasing the King's hunting grounds in the Alps to Italy, or military assistance from England, are mooted.

At Preslin's, Anne insists on not being left alone, and so accompanies Steven to the Abbot's. In council, de Coligny insults the Queen Mother in her presence, earning her enmity, Tavannes' rage and the King's favour.

Steven arrives at the Abbot's house and is finally shown into his presence. He pretends he has brought the runaway Anne back to the house, earning the Abbot's favour. Tavannes arrives to discuss the conspiracy, and from incautious words spoken by the Abbot Steven realises that it is the Admiral who is going to be killed, and today, on his way back from the council meeting at the Louvre. Steven heads to the Admiral's house and tells Nicholas of the conspiracy against his master.

Bondot shoots at de Coligny in the street, but at the last moment the Admiral stoops to pick up a piece of paper, and the shot only wounds him, rather than kills him.

Colbert brings news of the failure to kill de Coligny, and in a rage Tavannes instructs the guard to kill the Abbot.

De Teligny reports the news of the attempt to kill the Admiral to the Queen Mother and the King at the Louvre; the King is enraged.

De Coligny, at his own house, waits for a surgeon, while Steven explains the plot against the Admiral to Nicholas. Nicholas blames the Abbot but Steven insists that the Abbot is definitely the Doctor

'Now I've seen him I'm sure of it.' De Teligny arrives and tells Nicholas that the Abbot has been murdered by 'some of our men', i.e. Huguenots, as a reprisal for the attack on the Admiral, and then returns to the Louvre.

There, the King makes Tavannes responsible for de Coligny's safety and declares himself sick of both sides in the religious argument: He demands to be left alone, but his mother refuses and admits to him that she and Tavannes were responsible for the attack on de Coligny. She tells the King that his Huguenot subjects do not care for his protection and would rather have Henry of Navarre as their King. She shows him a list which she says is of prominent Catholics the Huguenots are planning to kill, including herself.

Steven, outside the Abbot's house, finds the Abbot's body and believes it to be the Doctor's. He is chased away from the house by a mob who believe that he is a Huguenot and was responsible for the Abbot's death.

In the very first scene of 'Priest of Death' Steven, jokingly yet specifically, draws Anne's, and thus the audience's, attention to how the complex clothing requirements of 16th-century society make identification of the individual difficult. It's an interesting grace note on the story's games with identity and identification.

This episode is less circumlocutionary than 'The Sea Beggar', although Steven does engage in another loop from Preslin's, back to the Abbot's then to the Admiral's then back to the Abbot's again, and de Teligny is left by the demands of the plot to bounce from the Louvre to the Admiral's house and back again. While at the Louvre he makes a joke about French bears not wishing to be leased to be hunted by Italians, which again flags up the themes of identity with which the serial concerns itself, and in an amusing way.

At the beginning of the episode Steven says he is 'Almost certain...' that the Doctor is the Abbot. When both Steven and the audience hear the Abbot speak for the first time, his warbling delivery does not seem at all Doctorish, except once, briefly, when he expresses anger at Colbert, and Hartnell's performance is a significant departure from how he plays the Doctor. (Director Paddy Russell would later comment that on this episode:

> 'I had the natural advantage with Bill, with whom I got on very well, in terms of saying "The Doctor's showing" if I didn't like what he was doing. That worked like a charm, because the Doctor couldn't show.'[34])

Despite this, Steven becomes **more, not less,** convinced that the Abbot is the Doctor after meeting him, and becomes so sure of his identity that he betrays Anne to him, thinking it will not matter. This crucial misjudgement could easily have resulted in the girl's death, and yet she never mentions it afterwards. (Anne disappears from the episode after this scene, presumably she has gone back to Preslin's, and she does not mention it next week.) Having become wholly convinced that the Abbot is the Doctor, Steven is understandably distraught when he finds the old man's corpse in the street.

The two scenes in which the Abbot appears (alive) in this episode lead into one another, without him leaving Tavannes' sight

---

[34] Marson, Richard, 'Paddy's Field! Paddy Russell Interview'. DWM #127.

between them, and the second ends with his death. This means that at no point in 'Priest of Death' is 'the Abbot' actually the Doctor in disguise. It is also unlikely that the Abbot's single scene in 'The Sea Beggar' was the Doctor pretending to be him, as the hunt for Anne is something that the real Abbot is concerned with, whereas in 'War of God' the Doctor left the Inn before she arrived and when he returns in 'Bell of Doom' he twice demonstrates no knowledge of, or interest in, her.

Thus in the televised *The Massacre* the Doctor does not impersonate the Abbot, unless he does so off-screen, nor does he seem to learn of their resemblance until minutes before the serial's conclusion. There is no justification within the narrative for the Doctor and the Abbot resembling one another, nor is there any attempt to either supply one or excuse its absence[35].The Abbot, in the end, is less than he appears to both Steven and the audience. He is simply an arrogant ('Of course, I never fail, and neither do my servants') and incompetent (he does and they do) churchman, who fails in his allotted tasks due to his own shortcomings and is killed

---

[35] Steven Moffat, **Doctor Who**'s Executive Producer and Head Writer from 2010 to the present, has more than once publicly implied that the fact that various incarnations of the Doctor, not merely Hartnell's but also Troughton's, Colin Baker's and Peter Capaldi's, have doppelgangers across time and space may form a plot-point in **Doctor Who** at some future point; which would constitute an extraordinary use of **Doctor Who**'s (arguable) nature as a single vast text. An element of this may be seen in the 2015 episode *The Girl Who Died*. (See also Appendix 2: The Family Chaplet.)

for this on Tavannes' orders. His resemblance to the Doctor is a coincidence[36].

Until the character's corpse is seen, this is ambiguous, but is so almost entirely from the perspective of the audience and their identification character Steven. (Tavannes has lines which are clearly meant to hint to the audience that the Abbot is the Doctor, disrupting the Marshall's plans from within[37], but from Tavannes' own perspective it is simply another reference to the Abbot's ineptitude, something he has been worrying about since the first time he spoke about him.) This ambiguity has been sustained in the collective mind of **Doctor Who** fans, the serial's only ongoing audience, for decades after its definitive resolution at the end of 'Priest of Death'. This is in part because of the inability to see the serial, and in part because of the novelisation's primacy amongst this audience.

Within the overall story structure of *The Massacre*, the moment in 'War of God' where Colbert bumps into the Doctor has now been forgotten. It is a plotting red herring, part of the indeterminacy

---

[36] The serial's credits accord with this view, mostly. Hartnell is credited as 'Dr Who' on the first and last episodes and as 'Abbot of Amboise' on the middle two instalments. This might be seen as an attempt to clarify matters, but unless the man who appears in the final scene of 'War of God' is the Doctor pretending to be the Abbot, Hartnell plays both parts in that episode, but is only credited for one. (The PasB for the episode credits him as both characters. *Radio Times* credits him as 'Dr Who' on all four episodes and 'The Abbot of Amboise' on the middle two.)

[37] E.g. 'It is strange, Father Abbot, that since you came everything that has been so carefully planned has gone wrong'.

over the Abbot's identity that ceases to have any utility once the character is dead. (A retrospective application of Occam's razor would suggest that Colbert simply began to enter the Tavern, presumably either to meet or because he was looking for Duval, who had been there until minutes earlier; noticed that the clientele consisted largely of Huguenots, including the notorious Lerans; and quickly departed for the Abbot's house. In terms of the events of 'War of God', Colbert's near entrance to the tavern is before Anne Chaplet's panicked escape from the Abbot's house, so he cannot be looking for her.)

Colbert disappears from the serial at the end of this episode. This is partially a function of the serial's once-a-week-recording production process (had Christopher Tranchell appeared in even one scene of 'Bell of Doom' he would have to be paid for another week's work and attend another episode recording), but it may also indicate that the utility of the character ends when the 'Is the Abbot the Doctor?' question is resolved. It is possible, given the speed with which Tosh (estimates he) redrafted the episodes, that the early instalments were written ambiguously so that decisions as to exactly what happens to who and when could be made during the redrafting of the later ones, without having to return to the earlier episodes. He may have left himself options. The doubt over the Abbott's identity is a complicated question with a simple but largely unsatisfying answer, which is perhaps what should be expected from an extemporised plot thread.

Tavannes has already made the audience aware of the Queen Mother's implication in the plot to kill de Coligny, but here she confesses her culpability to her son and the audience, designating it 'duty'. Catherine tells her son that the Calvinist Navarre is now 'in sight of the throne' because of his marriage to Margaret. But Navarre's position as heir to the Crown of France (he was then fourth in line, behind Charles' two younger brothers, Henry and Hercule Francois) was in no way based on his marriage to Margaret. As an agnatic descendent of Louis IX of France, his claim rested on the blood in his own veins. (He is also consistently referred to throughout the serial as a Prince, when he was already a King. Navarre was a separate Kingdom in its own right. The crowns of Navarre and France combined when this Henry, the III of Navarre, became Henry IV of France in 1589. The use of 'Prince' to mean 'ruler' was not uncommon in 16th-century English, but that is not how it is used here.)

Although they both were dead before 40 (Henry III was murdered, whereas Hercule Francois, who never ascended the throne, died of malaria, probably contracted on the battlefield in the Netherlands), in 1572 Charles IX's younger brothers were healthy young men (in contrast to the King himself, who had often been sickly) and the youngest was a suitor for the hand of Elizabeth I of England, a marriage that would have probably seen any offspring unite the English and French thrones. (Hercule Francois had suffered smallpox as a child; it left him scarred, but not physically incapacitated. Given that Hercule Francois, as Catherine had long feared he might, joined the rebels in a later stage of the Wars of Religion, and fought at Navarre's side against his Mother and brother's troops, it is odd that he does not warrant the smallest mention in Catherine's screed as to the succession here.)

This is also strange from a plotting perspective. In the serial Catherine is portrayed as having both created the treaty of religious toleration that Tavannes despises, and arranged the marriage of

54

her daughter to Navarre. It is this marriage which she now tells her son is the reason that there needs to be a general slaughter of Huguenots. This means that the serial's Catherine either arranged the marriage without anticipating the consequences or arranged it solely as an excuse to create the Massacre. She has either been inching towards this mass murder for the best part of a decade, or has made a series of elementary errors of policy that have placed her in a position where she is reacting murderously to her own mistakes.

Bell of Doom

23 August 1572

Anne has spent a second night in Preslin's shop, this time alone. Steven arrives and explains that he spent the night hiding from the authorities. He is convinced that the Doctor is dead and after considering options for his future, initiates a search for the TARDIS key, believing the Doctor's clothes to be in Preslin's shop[38].

Queen Catherine informs Marshall Tavannes that a general massacre of Protestants within Paris is to be initiated on the King's instructions. Tavannes forces the Queen to see that Navarre cannot be among those killed. The death of 'a Protestant prince' would provoke war. She reluctantly concurs.

---

[38] Steven's belief that the Doctor's clothes must be in Preslin's shop would make more sense if they had been there together at some point in the preceding two episodes. Is this plot movement perhaps left over from Lucarotti's draft?

The Doctor arrives at Preslin's shop. He is not dead, and will only say that he was 'unavoidably delayed', giving no further or more coherent reasons for his absence. On finding out the date he sends Anne away and explains that he and Steven must leave in the TARDIS at once.

Tavannes informs Duval that they can go ahead with a general massacre, rather than the more targeted set of killings they had planned, but that Duval's role will be to escort Henry of Navarre out of the city and to safety.

Once they have departed in the TARDIS, the Doctor explains to Steven that Paris is about to see tens of thousands of its Huguenot inhabitants dies at the hands of their Catholic fellow citizens. The Doctor and Steven quarrel, with Steven insisting that the Doctor sent Anne to her death. Steven walks out of the ship at the first place it arrives.

Left alone, the Doctor contemplates the nature of his lifestyle and the friends and companions he has lost. The Doctor is then interrupted by the arrival of the teenaged Miss Dorothea Chaplet. Steven returns and the TARDIS departs with all three on board. The Doctor notes that Dorothea looks like his granddaughter Susan, while Steven speculates that she may be a descendant of Anne's, thus proving that she survived the slaughter at which she was left.

When the Doctor returns to Preslin's empty shop, he simply asserts to Steven and Anne that Preslin is not, as they suspect, 'dead or in prison'. There is no further explanation or adumbration of where he has been. Lucarotti has described this sequence thus:

> '...one of the most unforgivable bits is where the Doctor reappears and Steven asks where he's been and the

Doctor says "Doesn't matter, dear boy, you'd never understand," and that's supposed to explain his absence for three episodes.'[39]

The most obvious conclusion the audience must reach, from the little information the episode gives them, is that the Doctor has spent the interceding 72 hours arranging Preslin's exit from Paris and then escorting him out of the city[40]. Quite how is never even hinted at, but it was not by impersonating the Abbot, unless he did so entirely off-screen.

The Doctor here demonstrates no knowledge of the Abbot's death or the plot to kill de Coligny with which the Abbot was concerned. This could be an affectation, but the horror with which he reacts when he discovers the month and year seem to rule that out. He even seems to have no knowledge of the Abbot's physical resemblance to him. (He simply does not react to Steven's comment 'The Abbot really did look like you' **at all**.)

The Doctor's advising Anne to 'Stay indoors tomorrow' to avoid being murdered is odd considering the nationwide Massacre continued for months, although his comment that the guards will have 'other things on their mind tonight' than searching the streets for her is true. The killings on the night of 23 and 24 August were largely of high-ranking Huguenots, many inside the Louvre or the

---

[39] Russell, 'Off The Shelf'.

[40] As to why it has taken so long, I might only semi-seriously suggest that he has also been participating in the events of *The Three Doctors* (1972-73). But such metafictional retcons are (largely) outside the assumed scope of this essay.

Admiral's house; the mass extermination of the general population only began in earnest on the morning of the 24th.

Tavannes persuades Catherine to spare Navarre by arguing that his death would provoke an international war, with France as one of the combatants. The moment is rather thrown away, but Catherine's quick acquiescence to the point makes sense. She has repeatedly argued, as has Tavannes, that aiding 'the Dutch' 'against Spain' is beyond France's financial resources. As presumably would be a defensive war against the combined powers of Protestant Europe. It is an opportunity, partially eschewed, to show a more nuanced Catherine, who is in part genuinely motivated by financial and diplomatic concerns, rather than sectarian bloodlust.

CHAPTER 3: DIFFERENCES IN RELIGION

'You'll only be found out for the man that you are,' the Doctor tells Steven Taylor, Pilot of the Future but honorary man of the 1960s, before departing from the tavern in 'War of God'. Within minutes the Doctor's prediction is proven correct. From then, until the Doctor himself explains what has transpired in the TARDIS three episodes/weeks/days later, Steven is never not at sea. Steven's absolute ignorance of the period drives and defines his every action in the story. Even at a physical level, his inability to navigate Paris' geography without help is repeatedly drawn attention to and, across the middle two instalments of the serial, leads to scenes where he wanders the streets hoping to be spotted by someone else relevant to the plot. (Conveniently, on at least two separate occasions, he is.)

Steven also lacks a clear understanding that Paris is a city with a strictly patrolled curfew, which prompts him to remain at the tavern until far later than is advisable. The means that he stays at the Admiral's house overnight, something that happens simply because he sees Nicholas as the curfew approaches. Had Steven understood the curfew, let alone what will transpire in 72 hours, he might have returned to where the TARDIS is, despite not having a key. (The ship is well hidden.) But simply going home with Nicholas leads others to see him as aligned with the Huguenot faction in French religious politics.

He becomes partisan **by accident**.

Dialogue in the script declares Steven to be both English and a Protestant, but Peter Purves' delivery softens both of these revelations, and it is possible from his reading of the line that Steven is simply saying what others want to hear. Muss assumes that an Englishman must be 'for the Huguenot' because the Church of England is, like the French reform movement of the 1570s, theologically Calvinist (this remains true, which is often a surprise even to people active within it). Steven, though, shows no hint of understanding this, let alone that theology is something that ordinary people will literally kill, and die, for in the world in which he has found himself.

I do not propose to write a history of the reformation in France[41], or claim to be capable of doing so, but a little (**hugely** simplified and adulterated) historical context is required here. The 16th century saw the emergence of several movements across Europe which were later grouped together as 'Protestant'. These are seen as evolving out of the Humanist movement, which emphasised textual engagement and critical thinking. (Although there were, of course, many Catholic Humanists, e.g. Sir Thomas More, who was so Catholic he was eventually canonised.) These movements looked to 'reform' Christianity which, in the form of the Roman Catholic Church, they saw as having lost its way and having drifted, by accident or design, from that which the Bible (emphasised as the source of all worldly authority for Christians) described, permitted or designated as true.

---

[41] Mack P Holt's *The French Wars of Religion, 1562-1629* is an accessible, yet scholarly, single-volume history of its topic that in addition contains much well-explained contextual material on the French Reformation. Those intrigued by the topic are directed to it.

The French-born theologian John Calvin (1509-1564) was of the second generation of 16th-century reformist thinkers; 'Huguenot' was the initially derisory term applied in France, by the French, to those whose religious practices and beliefs were derived, directly or indirectly, from Calvin's writings. By the middle of the 16th century in France they formed a sizeable minority, which was mostly concentrated in certain specific areas, geographically speaking.

The French state was Catholic, with its King bearing the ancient title 'Most Christian King' – bestowed by the Pope in perpetuity centuries before – and, by the middle 16th century, a significant role in 'guiding' the Church, up to and including control over the appointment of senior churchmen.

From 1562 to 1629 a series of civil wars were fought in France over the religious differences between the Huguenot minority and the Catholic majority, in which ideas of religious reform, territorial self-determination and monarchical authority cross-pollinated[42]. (In the 16th century the noun 'religion' designated as much a group of people as it did a body of thought.)

August 1572 fell during the peace following what is usually called the Third of the French Wars of Religion. This had ended in August

---

[42] Calvinist thinking was, by the 1570s, drifting in a direction which, while not exactly republican, held that Kings held their authority as much from the people they ruled as from the God who had appointed them.

1570 with the Peace of Saint-Germain[43], a treaty signed by the King, Charles IX, on the part of the state and by Gaspard II de Coligny on part of the Huguenots. The treaty contained numerous concessions concerning freedom of worship for the minority and, crucially, provisions to punish Catholics who did not extend freedom of religion to them. It also allowed Coligny's faction to retain administrative control of certain cities and towns that had been taken by force during the war, including four strategically key fortified towns: La Rochelle, La Charité, Cognac and Montabaun. Huguenots were permitted to openly hold public office in France and (eventually after a decent interval of a year or so) Coligny was, as seen in the story, given a place on the King's council and made Admiral of France. It was an office with a substantial stipend attached to it, along with its political and military clout.

The concessions to the Huguenots led a faction of Catholic nobles, loosely organised around the Guise family, to temporarily quit the King's court and council, and in early 1572 it was announced that the King's sister Margaret would, that summer, be married to King Henry of Navarre. Meanwhile the Queen Mother continued to negotiate to marry her youngest son, Hercule Francois, to the (ambiguously) Calvinist Queen Elizabeth of England.

This was an environment in which a feeling quickly emerged, shared by the both the Guise faction, who quickly returned to court, and the ordinary and overwhelmingly Catholic people of France, that the Huguenots were over-indulged by the treaty of

---

[43] This is the 'treaty negotiated by the Queen Mother... generous in the extreme to the Free Thinkers' that Tavannes mentions in 'The Sea Beggar'.

1570 – particularly when measures were taken by the state actively to enforce the Edict's provisions punishing Catholics for not showing due toleration. These including removing street furniture, such as the Cross on the Rue St-Denis, a monument that marked the house of two Huguenot preachers killed by a mob in 1569. It was not a monument to fallen, but a celebration of Paris' victory over heresy. It was removed under heavily armed guard, on the King's direct personal instruction and over the objections of the Paris municipal authorities, in December 1571. The occasion prompted a riot in which dozens died. There were many similar 'small' incidents[44].

The serial stages its own iterations of these events, in order to emphasise that atmosphere in Paris in August 1572. It partially does so by having a large number of speaking but unnamed characters, everymen and women, who largely appear only in one scene each, but who each convey at different times the feeling of what Gaston calls 'the common people of Paris'. They seem to function, in so far as we can tell in the absence of images, as a kind of chorus, although in a sense that seems more reminiscent of the didactic work of the Berliner Ensemble than classical Greek drama. (This is not as much of a leap as it may at first seem; director Paddy Russell had worked on television adaptations of plays originally staged by the Berliner Ensemble which retained the company's *Verfremdungseffekt* techniques; indeed they do so to the extent that members of the crew, including Russell herself, are seen on screen at key moments.)

---

[44] As indeed the serial's Tavannes notes in 'Priest of Death'.

The woman Steven and Nicholas encounter outside Preslin's shop is very quick to explain to complete strangers that Preslin was not merely likely burnt but that, if he was not, then he should have been. A more extreme example is seen when the small crowd that sees the Abbot's corpse at the end of 'Priest of Death' are willing, on no evidence at all, to chase Steven with what the script explicitly calls murderous intent, on the off chance that he: a) is a Huguenot, which is possible, and b) has killed a priest. A more low-key one is how the landlord of the tavern is suddenly wholly uninterested in Steven's plight simply because he associates him with the Huguenots.

These are the ordinary people of Paris. Not unreasonable ordinarily, but capable of a terrible fervour when matters of Christianity are broached. This is necessary in order for the story's climax to make any sense to the viewer, of course, but it is accomplished in such a way as to make clear that this is 'normal', that in this time and place, 'Protestants and Catholics alike... each viewed the other as pollutants of their own particular notion of the body social'[45].

The serial's Catherine tells Tavannes, 'The good people of Paris know their enemies'[46]; she understands that the public distinction between factions has sufficiently othered them from each other's perspective, that violence is never far below the surface and that this is accompanied by an absolute conviction of the morality of such violence: 'Here in Paris, we know what is right' the Landlord of the Inn confides to Duval, in the same conversation in which he

---

[45] Holt, Mack P, *The French Wars of Religion, 1562-1629*, Chapter 3.
[46] 'The Sea Beggar'.

casually comments 'I hate these Huguenots as much as the next man'.

These attitudes are not confined to hoi polloi and unnamed characters: Simon Duval (a man who will, three episodes later, express an almost sexual thrill at the possibility that he will be given 'the honour' of killing Navarre with his own hands) is polite and pleasant to Steven when he encounters him at the end of 'War of God', but once he has coded Steven as 'for the Huguenot' he is the enemy. Even Gaston, a character we are largely encouraged to like, thinks it would be entirely reasonable to kill Steven in cold blood on the suspicion of him being a Catholic spy, and later reproaches himself for not having the courage to do so when given the opportunity.

This absence of fellow-feeling has been seen by historians of the period as the key to understanding the Massacre as a violent, murderous expression of the religious divide of early modern France:

> '[the key is] not so much [..] the appalling tragedies involved as their demonstration of the power of sectarian passion to break down the barriers of civilisation, community and accepted morality... Christians massacring other Christians, who were not foreign enemies but their neighbours, with which they and their forebears had lived in a Christian community, and under the same ruler, for a thousand years.'[47]

---

[47] Koenigsberger, H G, *Early Modern Europe 1500 - 1789*, p115.

This is the situation, almost to the day, in which Steven finds himself, armed with even less information than the over-tidied version above, and without even enough context to know what a 'Sea Beggar' is.

STEVEN

I knew that the Sea Beggar was going to be killed. Until this morning I didn't know who that was.

MUSS

I could've told you. How did you find out?[48]

In plot terms, Muss is referring to his conversation with de Coligny at the end of the previous episode, in which the Admiral announced that the King had given him such a title. This is structurally odd. 'The Sea Beggar' is the code name given to de Coligny by the conspiracy to assassinate him, which consists of Tavannes, Duval, Amboise and Colbert, all working towards the Queen Mother. Unless we are to accept that the King too is involved in the conspiracy (which would make his public rage in 'Priest of Death' play-acting, and his private comments somewhere between advanced hypocrisy and multiple personality disorder, which is too hard a counter-reading to be reasonably considered) then the King independently bestows the phrase, as a nickname, on de Coligny for no purpose other than for the audience to find out that Gaspard de Coligny and the Sea Beggar are one and the same at the end of the second episode, and for Nicholas to then discover the same part way through 'Priest of Death'. This rather suggests

---

[48] 'Priest of Death'.

that, if it is such an obvious nickname for de Coligny that the King can bestow it publicly and independently of his mother and the conspirators, then it's a **terrible** code name. (This can perhaps be explained in terms of the Abbot's general ineptitude, but the serial itself does not choose to.) Steven is not only incapable of parsing the codename into something recognisable, he doesn't have any context into which to place the term. The audience have at least been told by de Coligny himself that 'the Sea Beggars' is a term for 'the Dutch'[49].

More specifically, it was a term for Calvinist-inspired privateers that acted as naval forces for the (Calvinist) aristocracy of much of the 17 northern European provinces (collectively referred to as the Low Countries) in their revolt against the (Catholic) government of Imperial Spain, the King of which, Philip II, had inherited them from his father Charles. (Indeed, the lyric 'I have always honoured the King of Spain' remains in the Dutch national anthem to this day.)

Charles had himself acquired these territories in his capacity as Holy Roman Emperor, rather than as King of Spain (he held both offices, which was not normally the case for one individual). In 1549 Charles' administrators had reorganised these 17 provinces into something resembling a single unit, unifying many laws and abolishing local customs, but there was not a single, unified 'Netherlands' nation state analogous to the modern Kingdom of the Netherlands. (It must be stressed that political Low Countries of the 16th century incorporated land that is now in Belgium and Austria.)

---

[49] 'The Sea Beggar'.

An armed revolt, which de Coligny simply calls the 'fight with Spain'[50] began in 1568, four years before the story is set, and would continue, with occasional periods of peace, for another 80 years. (Seven of these provinces, styling themselves 'The United Provinces', declared themselves wholly independent of Spain in 1579, becoming the predecessor of the later Dutch Republic and the modern day Kingdom of the Netherlands, but Spain did not acknowledge this until 1648. The other 10 provinces remained under direct Spanish control, before being ceded to Austria in 1714, then conquered and annexed by the First French Republic in 1795, and reunited with the rest of the Netherlands in 1815, before they split away from it in 1830 to become something resembling modern Belgium.)

Tavannes believes that de Coligny's sympathy for the Dutch is motivated purely by their being his co-religionists, but de Coligny himself articulates a belief that war against Spain would unite all the peoples of France in a single common endeavour against an external foe. (Interestingly, an almost identical plot element is present in the preceding **Doctor Who** serial *The Daleks' Master Plan*. As it seems likely the historical Coligny did believe this, and given Donald Tosh had at least some role in redrafting both stories, it is likely the idea was cross-pollinated to *Master Plan* either from *The Massacre* itself or Tosh's research for it.)

It is typical of the serial's ambiguous portrayal of religious partisanship that we have a situation where Tavannes, who is religiously motivated[51], assigns a religious motivation to de

---

[50] 'The Sea Beggar'.
[51] Or at least is as portrayed in the serial.

Coligny's actions. This **is** part of the serial's de Coligny's motivation, but not the **whole** of it. The scripts' Tavannes has a layered approach to religion, politics and death. He is engaged in a long-gestating conspiracy to murder a political rival with whom he is on polite, even friendly, speaking terms. (They share a barbed joke, or at least a moment of understanding, about the difficulty of meeting with the Queen Mother.) Yet he is moved to eloquent tears by the prospect of thousands of Huguenots dying on the streets of Paris, despite having been delighted by the possibility of dozens dying within the corridors of the Louvre. He himself articulates his motivation, shared with the Queen Mother, as being 'fear of a Protestant France'[52], but there are clearly limits to what he is prepared to do to avoid one. He is also quite capable of ordering the extrajudicial murder of a senior Catholic churchman in front of witnesses, indicating a somewhat flexible approach to venerating those in the service of his own faith.

Tavannes refers to the Catholic mob that will shortly murder thousands, in the name of a religion he shares with the killers, as 'the wolves of Paris'[53]. In this particular context his comment calls to mind Saint Augustine's comment on how, judged as God will judge them **by their actions**, many ostensibly good Catholics are not as secure in salvation as they themselves assume. Or as he expressed it: 'How many sheep there are without, how many wolves within!'[54]

---

[52] 'Bell of Doom'.
[53] 'Bell of Doom'.
[54] St Augustine, *Tractates on the Gospel of John*, 45.12.

Is *The Massacre* wholly innocent of anti-Catholicism itself? That might seem like an odd question to ask about something which dramatizes an event in which thousands of non-Catholics died, killed by Catholics on the orders of (someone within) the Catholic hierarchy, but it is worth asking. Unconscious anti-Catholicism has long been prevalent in England and Wales[55], part of an English-language tradition that casually conflates the concepts of the Renaissance with the English Reformation and the emergence of the nation state.

Certainly there are arguments to be made about the titles of the episodes. 'Priest' is a term generally eschewed by Protestant denominations and here it is paired with 'Death'; and while the 'Bell of Doom' of the fourth episode's title is that of the curfew, historically it is also that of the Catholic cathedral of Notre Dame. The ringing of small bells during the Eucharist, accompanied by the release of incense, is a Catholic ritual that gifted the derogatory term 'smells and bells', which remains common to describe Catholic celebration.) Both titles link symbols of Catholicism with destruction, whereas the second episode's title concerns the Huguenot de Coligny, who is portrayed as a brave, selfless and learned man who, even when mortally wounded, is more concerned with the fate of his co-religionists than his own survival.

The script is also keen to align Huguenotism exclusively with the 'New Learning' and Renaissance Humanism. The term 'Free Thinkers' is used liberally in the teleplay, always in relation to the Huguenots, and in 'War of God' the Catholic Church, or at least its

---

[55] It generally finds more overt expression in Scotland and Northern Ireland.

representative the Abbot of Amboise, is shown to be persecuting the apothecaries for their interest in science, rather than for religious reasons.

STEVEN

Yes. You see, he's gone to find an apothecary there.

MUSS

Is he sick?

STEVEN

Oh, no, no, no. He's a scientist. He's gone to talk to him about his idea.

MUSS

A dangerous thing to do in days like these.

This portrays the Catholic Church as being inherently reactionary with regard to scientific method as well as partisan in theology, whereas Protestantism is seen to be aligned with these progressive or empirical forces. (There is a complex discussion to be had about the role of religious organisations of many stripes in patronising or retarding scientific development s in the early modern period, but to even begin it would absorb the remaining word count of this essay without trying.) In Lucarotti's novelisation (p40) Preslin is explicitly a Protestant, but this is not the case in the teleplay where the idea he has heretical beliefs is only articulated by a passer-by, and where it is explicitly his scientific interests that are heretical, not his views on, for example, real presence in the Eucharist. The novelisation also links Preslin's persecution with real-life 16th-century laws prohibiting non-Catholics from practicing in certain professions, including as an apothecary. Again, these details are nowhere found in the teleplay.

It is also interesting that 'A Chaplet' is, as well as being Anne's name, a kind of prayer using rosaries or other sacramental beads. It is uncommon in 'reformed' churches and certainly antithetical to Calvinism, but very common in Catholicism and 'higher' forms of Protestantism, including variations within Anglicanism. Anne's family is from the highly Catholic area of Lorraine, and her surname could indicate a very recent conversion by her family to reformed religion. It is striking thematically, given the civil nature of the religious warfare in the story, to give a persecuted Huguenot a name derived from Catholic devotionals.

We should not make too much of this. These are cultural assumptions rather than overt prejudice, and the scripts are more balanced elsewhere. Lerans is a bigoted roustabout, by his own admission constantly on the lookout for opportunities to 'bait a Catholic'[56]. He is also utterly contemptuous of the lower orders, announcing that 'No one is more ignorant than the common people of Paris'[57] and calling Anne a 'nothing' despite her being one of his co-religionists[58]. Class prejudice, it seems, trumps religious fellow-feeling. (He has no interest in Anne's plight until it is clear it intersects with his sectarian interests.) Lerans also rejects Nicholas' assertion that 'many of our followers are just as bad'[59] as the Catholics when it comes to sectarian violence. From this

---

[56] 'War of God'.
[57] 'War of God'.
[58] 'The Sea Beggar'.
[59] 'The Sea Beggar'.

perspective it is a shame that the transmitted version does not make more of the Amboise connection. There a Huguenot mob did cause massive damage and considerable loss of life. (Additionally, while Paddy Russell's direction, in so far as can be told from audio recordings, cannot be faulted, it is interesting to wonder what director John Crockett, who had worked on Lucarotti's previous **Doctor Who** serials, would have made of *The Massacre*. Crockett left television and devoted his life to Catholicism, living, dying and being buried in Prinknash Abbey, Stroud.)

Steven's consistent ignorance of the details of theological division in early modern France is inevitably going to be shared by some of the serial's audience, for they are never wholly articulated by the piece. This is not merely because theology is complex. The musical *Les Misérables* constructs its narrative as a contrast between determinist Huguenot and redemptive Catholic views of the world, represented by Javert and Valjean respectively, and this has been easily communicated to an international audience that now numbers in, at least, the tens of millions. (This overt juxtaposition is not drawn from Victor Hugo's original novel. Hugo was not exactly a friend to the Roman Catholic Church.)

Without wishing to caricature Calvinism or add thousands more to the billions of words already written discussing it, there are two key points of its theology that are specifically relevant to this serial. The first, and more complex, is that Calvinism holds that people are predestined either to be damned ('reprobate') or saved ('elect') and that no action they themselves take can alter that. This is the doctrine of Predestination. Salvation is indicated, but not prompted, by a person's faith; i.e., genuine religious faith is a consequence of having been preselected as one of God's elect, not a choice a human can make in order to achieve salvation.

This is a story about the inalterability of history and destiny in which several thousand members of a religious grouping **whose faith is specifically defined by adherence to a concept of predestination** are killed.

The second, and more simple point, is that Calvinism emphasises a human's personal relationship with the Christian God, one which does not require mediation through hierarchies or structures.

The Doctor and the Abbot are both real within the fiction. But on a metafictional level they are both the same person, in that they are both played by William Hartnell. It is not stretching the point to see the duplication of characters played by William Hartnell as serving the duality of Christian religion with which the serial concerns itself.

Both the Huguenot and Catholic figures spend 'The Sea Beggar' and 'Priest of Death' seeking the Abbot; the former because they believe he's the Doctor, and the latter because they lack faith in his abilities despite knowing him to be the Abbot. Throughout the televised story Steven struggles to reach the Abbot, believing him to be the Doctor and thus his salvation. His attempts to assert a personal relationship with this figure are wholly unsuccessful and very nearly get him killed. They do, or so it appears to Steven for nearly 24 anguished hours, get the Doctor killed.

Then, just when Steven is in absolute despair, the Doctor reappears. He is not dead. He was never dead. Steven was wrong. The Doctor was never a false Abbot. The Abbot was a false Doctor of Steven's own making. For Steven, the Doctor's reappearance is a resurrection. Until the old man walks into Preslin's shop, he is wholly convinced that the Doctor is dead and believes that he has seen his brutalised corpse.

Resurrection is the central mystery of all variations of Christianity. And *The Massacre* is a story explicitly concerned with variations in Christianity, which ends with the Doctor's apparent resurrection three days after the audience last saw him, and which begins with Steven being turned away from an Inn.

Just putting that out there.

The arrival of Dodo in the story's final scenes, a contemporary young woman whose existence is taken by both the Doctor and Steven to confirm Anne's survival, has been described as a 'redeeming... coda'[60]. Redemption in this sense, where human action can redeem prior human action, is a concept which the Calvinist form of Protestantism overtly and specifically disdains. As an idea it is profoundly Catholic.

The middle episodes then, dramatize the attempts to struggle towards God that divide the characters, and the last redeems Steven Taylor through the Doctor's resurrection and the Doctor through Anne's. This is a hugely interesting departure for **Doctor Who**, and if only Dodo and Anne were played by the same actress, the dramatic movement would be perfect. (The novelisation echoes this by noting that Dodo is Anne's 'double'[61]. On screen there is little obvious resemblance between the performers.)

---

[60] Cornell, Paul, Martin Day and Keith Topping, *Doctor Who: The Discontinuity Guide*, p52.
[61] Lucarotti, *Doctor Who: The Massacre*, p144.

The Massacre does not resolve the religious issues that power its drama any more than the bloody events with which it concludes resolved the religious divide of Early Modern France. (The present Fifth French Republic is an overtly secular state with no state religious institutions whatsoever, but the road to it from the ancient regime is not a smooth or easy one.) It does, however, discuss them, articulating the theological differences between Catholicism and Huguenotism, and dramatizing their dialogue, through character, theme and plot, and not merely in a literal manner.

Twenty-five years after his version of *The Massacre* wasn't made, Lucarotti wrote an interesting coda to the serial: a short prose fiction entitled 'Brief Encounter' and printed in *Doctor Who Magazine*. This features the author encountering the Doctor, characterised as played by Hartnell, in a French tavern. A notable feature of the story is the Doctor's total lack of interest in which religious faction the men he met belonged to, to the extent that he confuses which man was of which denomination and his misapprehension has to be corrected by Lucarotti.

A final note of interest in the story is that the script indicates that Nicholas and de Teligny 'kneel' by the Admiral's bed as he lies dying[62]. Is this missing scene **Doctor Who**'s most overt onscreen depiction of Christians at prayer?

---

[62] 'Bell of Doom'.

CHAPTER 4: DIFFERENCES ON HISTORY

It is routine for commentary on this **Doctor Who** serial to assume that the events portrayed within it aren't 'famous', or at least not when compared to those that form the basis of other 'past' **Doctor Who** serials; that it 'isn't about a well-known historical event'[63] and instead concerns one which is 'hardly in common cultural currency'[64]. But is the situation that clear-cut?

The event, after all, is a key one in the French Wars of Religion, and discussion of it was a feature of French public life well into the 20th century. Francois Mitterand, who was President of the French Republic until 1995, recalled the Wars of Religion being a daily matter of contention during his childhood, growing up Catholic in a part of France dominated by Huguenotism. Pope John Paul II apologised for, and condemned, the Massacre on behalf of the Catholic Church while visiting Paris on 23 August 1997.

The events of this serial have also been significant in (other) popular and enduring works of historical fiction. The Massacre is, in part, the topic of Dumas' *La Reine Margot* (1845). Significantly this is a novel which has never been out of print in English as well as French, and is itself the basis of two internationally celebrated film adaptations[65] of 1954 and 1994, the earlier of which was already well-known when this serial was written and produced.

---

[63] Sandifer, Phil, 'Not Always. I'm Sorry. (The Massacre)'.
[64] Tweed, Robert, 'The Massacre', *DreamWatch Bulletin* #117.
[65] There are multiple other adaptations, but those two are the key ones.

In addition, a section of D W Griffiths' 1916 film *Intolerance,* among the most admired and influential pictures of the silent era concerns the build up to the Massacre, while *The Massacre at Paris* is also the topic, and the most commonly used title, of one of the seven plays by the second most celebrated Early Modern English playwright, Christopher Marlowe. The fourth episode of BBC One's *Elizabeth R*, 'Shadow in the Sun' (1971), made five years later, similarly assumes the audience has some familiarity with the Massacre specifically and the French Wars of Religion more generally. (Incidentally, that episode was directed by Richard Martin, Verity Lambert's go-to director for 'blockbuster' **Doctor Who** serials, such as *The Dalek Invasion of Earth* (1964), *The Web Planet* (1965) and *The Chase*.)

The *Radio Times* article for the transmission of 'War of God' calls the events portrayed 'notorious'[66], indicating an assumption of familiarity with the topic, and clearly feels that mentioning the time and place is enough for the viewer to get by without any further glossing. These examples (and there are others) form a pattern of notable long-term engagement with the issues and events of the Massacre by Anglophone culture(s) in a way that writing about this **Doctor Who** serial has perhaps not quite synchronised with.

While it is arguable that the events are not as immediately notable to those outside France as the fall of Robespierre (the topic of the other 1960's **Doctor Who** serial set in France) they are also clearly of greater historical importance than some goings-on in a forgotten Aztec temple or the activities of a small group of smugglers in

---

[66] *Radio Times*, 5 to 13 February 1966.

Cornwall in a period so ambiguously portrayed it could be set at literally any point between 1670-1707 or 1714-30.

'Historically accurate' drama is, of course, impossible. Such fiction necessarily requires conflations, elisions and omissions. It will almost always involve taking sides, not necessarily in terms of partisanship, but in terms of interpretation. Performed drama collapses the multiple possibilities that can be presented in a piece of discursive writing about an event into a single mimetic depiction. No author can be blamed for this[67], but nevertheless the interpretation of events in *The Massacre*, if not their 'accuracy', requires some discussion.

Firstly, the serial indicates three times that 'the feast of Saint Bartholomew' is a major religious and public festival in France, with the King organising his council meetings around the date in 'Priest of Death', Tavannes referring to Bartholomew 'revelry' and Anne specifically referring to 'the celebrations' in 'Bell of Doom'. Yet, oddly, Saint Bartholomew's Day was **not** a substantial religious holiday in 16th-century France. It **was** the date of significant public revelry in the England of the same period, as celebrated in Ben Jonson's play *Bartholomew Fair* (1614) but not in France, either before or after the Massacre.

---

[67] It is a problem that disproportionately effects discussion of Doctor Who's early 'past' serials. No one wonders if King John was really impersonated by a robot, but if you point out that William de Preaux was kidnapped **after** John's brother King Richard suggested their sister Joanna marry Saphadin, not before, **Doctor Who** fans go quiet.

Secondly, as noted earlier, Charles Preslin is a fiction[68]. There were, however, significant figures in the French reformation, who were also practicing apothecaries, who would have been available to the story (regardless of who wrote it). Most notably, there is Pierre Touillet[69]. Touillet was a close associate of the more famous Jean Morely (1524-c1594), and a known associate of both Admiral de Coligny and Henry of Navarre's mother. Morely's father, also Jean, was the primary physician who attended on King Francis I, Catherine de Medici's father-in-law and grandfather to her sons, and the younger Jean moved in court circles early in life.

Touillet fled France after being summoned by the authorities and ordered to either justify or retract his repeating of Morely's own 'libel' concerning the Guise family and events in Amboise. (Broadly, he considered 'the Amboise conspiracy' a 'false flag' operation which was at least approved of by the Church.) Given this, it's hard to see how any real figure of the period could be more suited to the fictional Preslin's role in the story. As such, it is extremely tempting to speculate that Touillet fulfilled Preslin's role in Lucarotti's lost screenplay, but there is absolutely no evidence of this, and if he did Lucarotti had clearly forgotten him by 1987. (The serial also does not in any way acknowledge the philosopher Petrus Ramus, the protestant intellectual and university professor who is the Massacre's most famous individual victim, but while more

---

[68] Although he is perhaps named for the much later, and notorious, Parisian Charles Preslin (1804-47), whose fall from grace was instrumental in the collapse of the July Monarchy and the French Revolution of 1848.

[69] Kingdon, Robert McCune, *Geneva and the Consolidation of the French Protestant Movement, 1564-1572*, p65.

famous than Touillet, he would fit the story rather less well. Not least because history says he cannot be saved.)

Most importantly: a Cardinal of Lorraine is mentioned several times in *The Massacre*, but does not appear. (He is said to be in Rome, which the historical Cardinal was, in the summer of 1572.) This Cardinal (1524-74), whose forename was Charles, was a member of the Guise family and its aforementioned ultra-Catholic faction of the French nobility, who had fought alongside the Catholic crown in the earlier phase of the Wars of Religion, but who left the court following the peace of 1570.

It was, in part, the exit of the Guise family from frontline French politics that gave Coligny opportunities to influence the King's policy making. (Historians are, frankly, **very** divided on the extent to which he did.) The Guise family, the Cardinal aside, are not mentioned in the televised version of *The Massacre*.

In both versions of the story Anne is frightened into running away from the Cardinal of Lorraine's house by hearing men there talk of the religious violence at Vassy. Vassy (or Wassy) was not only a genuine event; it was the spark that lit the fire of the French Wars of Religion, and almost literally so at that. On 1 March 1562 a group of Huguenots were discovered worshipping within a barn that was within the Guises' lands. The then Duke, his son, his brother the Cardinal and members of their household burned down the barn with the congregation still inside it.

The serial puts the death count at a hundred, the novelisation a more conservative 25. Current estimates of the number of deaths vary, but it was certainly dozens, with many more injured. In the novelisation Anne describes climbing onto the roof of the burning building in order to avoid burning to death, a detail found in contemporary accounts of Vassy that is not found in the teleplay.

It is not a contrivance that a survivor of Vassy should be present in the Cardinal's household 10 years later when he himself was present at the event. The people of town were vassals of his nephew the Duke of Guise (his brother, the elder Duke, having died in the interim) and would and could be expected to form part of his household at his whim.

Moreover, in real life, Marmoutier Abbey and the area around Amboise were within the jurisdiction of the Cardinal of Lorraine. The institution's fictionalised Abbot being close to the Cardinal (he is his 'right hand'[70] and has 'worked for him for many years'[71]) is historically plausible, and a sudden appointment to this technically vacant office such as that implied in 'The Sea Beggar' would have been within the real-life Cardinal's gift, subject to royal approval.

This brings us to one of the strangest things about the serial; the complete absence of the Cardinal's nephew, the Duke of Guise, from events as portrayed onscreen. Coligny's would-be-assassin Maurevert was known to work for the Guise dynasty. The property from which he fired at the Admiral, and the horse on which he fled from the scene, were traced to the Guise family's ownership. This is why the Guise faction, rather than the Crown itself, is more normally considered to have arranged the initial assassination attempt on Coligny. It is not just a matter of circumstantial evidence, however: the Guise faction also had a motive.

---

[70] 'War of God'.
[71] 'The Sea Beggar'.

The Duke of Guise believed, and it is a belief that history finds credible, that Coligny had ordered the murder of his father. Duke Francis of Guise had been shot dead in cold blood at his base camp by John de Poltrot in 1563. Poltrot, a Huguenot, had gained access to the camp by subterfuge and in disguise, and he implicated Coligny in his plot when confessing. (This is, incidentally, something that the novel *La Reine Margot* notes on its first page, but which is not acknowledged by the 1954 film.) The Guise faction considered Francis' death to be an extrajudicial assassination, and as such not a legitimate action under the laws of arms. It was certainly the Duke of Guise who had Coligny killed on the night of 23 August, and almost certainly finished him off personally before abandoning his body to be mutilated by the mob, who hacked off his hands, feet, head and genitals, and sent at least some of them to the Pope as gifts. Mercifully, he seems never to have received them. For the Guises, the attempt to kill Coligny was as much about personality as politics, as well as being as much about politics as religion.

Does the serial avoid showing the Guise faction in order not to have to engage with these facts, or is it ignorant of them? The story firmly ascribes responsibility for both attacks on de Coligny to the Queen Mother. This **is** in accordance with at least some mainstream historical thinking at the time the serial was written[72], and *The Massacre* predates Nicola M Sutherland's magisterial source-based refutation of there being proof of Catherine's direct involvement with the shooting[73] by half a dozen years, but to

---

[72] Neale, J E, *The Age of Catherine de Medici*.
[73] Sutherland, Nicola M, *The Massacre of Saint Bartholomew and the European Conflict, 1559-72*, pp300-350.

completely absent the Duke, his family and their entire faction from the events of August 1572 is an extraordinary move, without precedent in drama about the event[74] and, notably, one not repeated by Lucarotti in his novelisation.

In the penultimate scene of 'Priest of Death' the Queen Mother shows the King a list[75], saying 'Look at these before you would decide who are your enemies. You think the Huguenots would stop at killing me? They want your blood too.' This is the only reference in the serial to one of the public justifications for the Massacre indulged in by the French state in its aftermath: that it was a pre-emptive response to an imminent attack on the state by Huguenots. (The King's most public response to the Massacre was to attend a Mass giving thanks that he had been saved from this plot by it.)

The historical consensus on the shooting of Coligny is that:

> 'whoever was implicated in the assassination plot... it was doubtless a plot to kill just one man – the admiral – not the first stage of something far more sinister. If a general massacre of those Huguenot nobles still in Paris after the wedding had been contemplated, it would have made no sense at all to alert them to the danger by singling out Coligny first.'[76]

---

[74] E.g. The Duke is one of the central characters of Marlowe's play, the first performances of which are recorded under the title *The Tragedy of the Guise*.
[75] 'Priest of Death'.
[76] Holt, *The French Wars of Religion*, Chapter 3.

Following the failure of the plot, the King's council met. Rumours were circulating that there would be reprisals from the Huguenot faction (to be clear, no coordinated reprisal was planned by the Huguenot faction, but there were certainly rumours of such a counter-strike that weekend), and the atmosphere was not helped by the fact that Charles de Teligny had an army 4,000 strong camped immediately outside Paris, something that is never mentioned in the serial.

A decision was made by the King's council to kill a large number of Huguenots, but even at this point, the hastily generated plan was to dispose of a few dozen significant figures, not to have one community of Paris murder several thousand people from another. Yet this is what the serial portrays. Four episodes of ambiguity, of convincing portrayals of a city on a knife edge of sectarian violence, are concluded with one person ordering the deaths of thousands, either on the spur of the moment or as the culmination of two years of work. It seems far more likely that the general Massacre erupted more or less spontaneously, the simmering tension of the previous two years exploding in response both to the court's simultaneous extrajudicial execution of dozens of prominent Huguenots, and the unjustified fears of reprisal from Teligny's army that had prompted them.

Just as Catherine de Medici's personal responsibility for the shooting of Coligny is in dispute, her responsibility for the Massacre, ordered at that council on the 23rd, is a matter of historical tradition, and widely adhered to, but it is one without contemporary documentary basis.

Given this, Tosh's confident assertion that his rewrites were inspired by a need 'not to show people like Catherine de Medici doing things they didn't do'[77] looks a little shaky. Frankly, we cannot be remotely certain of much of what Catherine de Medici did or did not do, only of what we cannot prove that she did (and indeed the small number of things we can prove that she did do).

We have already established that, in the serial, Catherine is not only personally responsible for ordering the Massacre, but organises, through Tavannes and the Abbot, the attack on de Coligny. This shooting occurs two days after he attends the marriage, which she had arranged, of her daughter to a prominent Protestant ally. This marriage was a response to a treaty between Catholic and Huguenot factions in France designed to end the religious civil war: a treaty that Catherine had also arranged.

The implication of the story, then, is that everything in this list is mere prologue to the Massacre. That Catherine has implemented a grandiose conspiracy over several years, and that her intention is to kill at least dozens, probably thousands. It seems that the terms of the peace, bringing de Coligny into the Louvre as a minister and the marriage itself, were all simply steps on a years-long road to this event, excuses to get the Huguenot leaders in Paris at the right time so they can unleash the mob.

In 'Bell of Doom' Tavannes says to Duval that 'Our plans for tomorrow can go ahead.' The Marshall has a list of those who are to die, and Duval is expecting to be given one, confirming the complicity of both not simply in the plan to kill the Admiral but also

---

[77] Hearn, 'Script Editing Who, Donald Tosh'.

in the contrivance of circumstances in which the Massacre can be staged. Did Catherine always intend a general Massacre, keeping this from Tavannes, who himself always intended merely a few dozen politically-expedient killings and thought the Queen Mother did likewise, or is the mass slaughter an innovation of the night of the 23rd?

The answer to this question is not fully articulated in dialogue in 'Bell of Doom' itself, but can perhaps be found earlier in the serial, and in plot motion rather than dialogue. In all versions of this story, Anne Chaplet runs away from the Abbot's house, in which she is a servant, because she overhears the Captain of the Guard discussing 'Vassy' and how 'it might happen again' and 'before the week was out'. The serial's Abbot is based in the Cardinal of Lorraine's house and the historical Cardinal's guard played a significant role in the real-life Massacre, including storming the Admiral's house and encouraging the violence that erupted outside it. If the Captain of the Cardinal's Guard is discussing Vassy and how 'it might happen again' and 'before the week was out' with the men who will actually implement the street violence when it happens, then it is more likely than not that a general Massacre has been planned and information about it is already passing in secret down the chain of command. Otherwise Anne coincidentally overhears a group of people who will, in three days' time, be ordered to conduct a massacre, casually discussing a massacre from 10 years before and how something like it may occur within a few days. Which seems **too** coincidental.

What Anne overhears in 'War of God' is also important when considering the idea that the serial's original audience would, due to a lack of historical knowledge, inevitably not have known that these episodes concluded in a (the) Massacre. This idea does somewhat founder on War of God's *Radio Times* entry making clear how this serial will end from the outset, but once Anne has reported what she has overheard, even those who do not read *Radio Times* have been told by the story itself, by dialogue from Anne and Nicholas and Gaston, that what Anne has run from is a conversation about the indiscriminate killing of a large number of people in the name of religion. It is not, although both Nicholas and Gaston convince themselves it is, a discussion of an attempt to kill a single prominent figure. It is talk of a massacre.

'Vassy', like 'Saint-Barthélemy', was an action prompted by the aristocracy in which many of the lower orders died. There is no such resemblance between 'Vassy' and the attempt on de Coligny's life to which the characters come to believe the conversation referred (and even less so the phantom plot to kill Navarre that Gaston convinces himself exists and which he mentions once in 'War of God' and once again in 'The Sea Beggar', another of the serial's structural oddities/red herrings).

Neither Gaston nor Nicholas can conceive of a massacre on the scale of the Massacre, because it has not happened yet. They simply do not consider even for a single a line of dialogue that the conversation they have had reported to them concerns the deaths of hundreds, let alone thousands; the intelligence they have must refer to politics, despite the reference to Vassy. Even to men familiar with Vassy, men who have fought in a religious war, something on the scale of the Massacre, inevitable to the audience, is literally unimaginable. This is, as well as another example of Gaston's classist failure to even consider the lives of the lower orders, the logic of tragedy in its most basic form: the characters charge towards a terrible conclusion that the audience can see but they cannot.

The assumption that the original audience cannot have known how the serial would conclude originates within the belief that the historical events the story is portraying are obscure. But even if that were true, Anne's nature as a survivor of Vassy and the plotline that unfurls from that are there to flag to the audience that a mass killing is imminent. We know, even though the characters do not, that there is more at stake than the life of one prominent man.

That Steven Taylor is ignorant of the events in which he is involved is, like his ignorance of Paris' religious distinctions, crucial to the way the story unfolds, but the serial itself does not assume an absolute ignorance of the topic in its audience. Rather, the serial assumes a general familiarity with these events, prods the audience carefully to remember them, and then uses Steven's lack of the same familiarity to create an unsettling atmosphere in which the audience, culturally forewarned in a way Steven is not, is partially complicit.

It is paradoxical that **Doctor Who** fan culture, informed of the serial's conclusion by the title given to it by posterity if nothing else, should collectively simultaneously praise the serial's forbidding atmosphere as it leads up to these events as a key quality of the piece, while assuming that the audience for whom it was written and made would have no idea that the story will end in tragedy.

The overall feeling of dread which permeates these episodes is perhaps their single most significant dramatic characteristic, and it is perhaps a misdiagnosis to both suggest that it is not a deliberate effect of the production and to imply that it is something that only a fan audience, working from an unanticipated sound recording in a future unimagined at the time of production, can fully engage with, due to access to historical information the original audience could not be expected to understand.

That the audience knows more than the characters by virtue of historical hindsight is one of the serial's most dramatic features, and it would not function as well without it. It may also be the reason that the serial chooses to portray the Massacre as the deliberate result of a long-gestating conspiracy, rather than as an exponentially increasing, but nevertheless spontaneous, series of acts of mob violence prompted by the murderous cover-up of a political failure.

While a long-gestating plan to kill thousands is less plausible historically, 'Bell of Doom''s brutal climax being the culmination of years of planning perhaps fits better with the serial's engagement with historical inevitability as a theme, even if this is achieved in a manner which slightly throws away the earlier episodes' portrayal of Paris as a sectarian tinder box. Nevertheless, this is the serial's interpretation of these historical events and it is entitled to it. However, it is hard not to conclude that 'Bell of Doom' clips the final hurdle in refuting a maxim attributed, almost certainly erroneously, to an author with whose work *The Massacre* frequently intersects, the elder Alexander Dumas: 'Never attribute to malice that which is more easily explained by incompetence.'[78]

---

[78] This phrase and variations on it are widely, and indeed wildly, attributed but it seems to be in point of fact a paraphrase of a translation of Goethe, whose epistolary novel *Die Leiden des Jungen* contains in its opening letter: 'Und ich habe, mein Lieber, wieder bei diesem kleinen Geschäft gefunden, dass Missverständnisse und Trägheit vielleicht mehr Irrungen in der Welt machen als List und Bosheit.' (Roughly 'And it seems to me, my love, that this small matter demonstrates that misunderstanding and neglect occasion more trials in the world than cunning and malice.')

CHAPTER 5: WHAT HAPPENED WITH *THE MASSACRE*?

'[He] offered to do a story about the Saint Bartholomew's Massacre, which I thought would be a marvellous idea.'[79]

'Unfortunately, I knew quite a lot about the Saint Bartholomew's Massacre and so when John delivered his scripts I looked through them and found that historically there were a lot of things wrong with them – I can't remember what now – but I had to change them...'[80]

'I had to go away and rewrite it from page one. Bill Hartnell was a good actor, and I wanted to give him something different to do. I gave Bill a doppelganger story where I got him to play the Abbot of Amboise, not just the Doctor. He had great fun doing it, as he wasn't having to learn all the usual scientific lines, as he had to do as the old man.'[81]

'I happened to see a copy of John's novelisation of *The Massacre* and he had based it on my revised scripts!'[82]

[Donald Tosh on *The Massacre*]

---

[79] Hearn, 'Script Editing Who, Donald Tosh'.
[80] Hearn, 'Script Editing Who, Donald Tosh'.
[81] Smith, 'Doctor Who story editor Donald Tosh'.
[82] Hearn, 'Script Editing Who, Donald Tosh'.

'Now, *The Massacre* had been imposed on me, I hadn't wanted to do it.'[83]

'The historical events described in *The Massacre* are factual, as were the 287 kilometres of tunnels and catacombs under Paris, some of which may still be visited. The woodcut engraving of the attempt on de Coligny's life, which shows a cowled cleric in a doorway, does exist. The author has seen it.'[84]

'Bill wanted a serial where we wasn't the Doctor, so we came up with the idea that he was the Abbot of Amboise, the Doctor's double.'[85]

'I explained that Donald Tosh, not I, had written it [the final episodes], and it [the book] couldn't be done like that, with the Doctor disappearing out of the story; he had to be involved, and in the book you could have the two stories. I had to then research the whole thing, so I went to Paris in January and discovered a lot of things about the period. Then I came to London for various things and then went to Paris and did more research and then began *The Massacre* as *The Massacre* is now [...] It took me about five months in all.'[86]

[John Lucarotti on *The Massacre*]

---

[83] Russell, 'Off The Shelf'.
[84] 'Author's Note' on the inside cover of the novel.
[85] Russell, 'Off The Shelf'.
[86] Russell, 'Off The Shelf'.

As you can see, Lucarotti and Tosh have independently offered incompatible recollections of the historical events surrounding the creation of this serial. Each, without reference to the other, denies the other's interpretation of those events, while both also claiming greater historical veracity for their own version of the narrative it contains, each denying the other's interpretation of **those** events.

This is, obviously, 'problematic'.

Lucarotti's novelisation is arguably **loosely** based on Tosh's revised scripts, in so much as they were the only scripts for the serial he had to hand when he wrote the book. It is certainly true that pages 11 to 50 of the novelisation[87] cover the same ground as the transmitted 'War of God' in plot terms, and the two pieces have almost identical scene breakdowns. (The serial begins on 20 August, whereas the novelisation presents roughly the same events as occurring on the 19th (p22).) As both tellings unfold over four days, this has the effect that the novelisation does not build up to the Massacre itself. Rather, the climactic event is the assassination attempt on de Coligny.)

In both tellings, these scenes feature the Doctor and Steven arriving in Paris and the Doctor deciding to visit Charles Preslin. There is then a visit to a tavern, where Gaston, Nicholas and Simon Duval are encountered for the first time, with the Doctor then heading to Preslin's shop, where he meets the apothecary, a persecuted and frightened man. Anne Chaplet escapes the house

---

[87] The numbered pagination of all three editions is identical, although Lucarotti's 'Author's Note', which is on a page before the numbering starts, is missing from the re-jacketed reprint of the paperback.

of the Abbot and relays her frightening information about Vassy. Her escape creates problems for Simon and her information causes concern for Gaston and Nicholas. Yet the dialogue in almost all these scenes is wholly different (except in the tavern, where it is largely the same as in the transmitted story).

Both versions end this section of the plot with the reveal of the Abbot's face. In the television version, the audience (but not Steven) sees that the Abbot either resembles the Doctor or is being impersonated by him. In the novelisation Steven sees the Abbot and thinks he is the Doctor, but the reader is already aware that the Abbot resembles the Doctor, and knows that the figure Steven has just glimpsed is the real Abbot, not the Doctor. (The Doctor has been taken into the tunnels beneath Paris by Preslin, and held thereagainst his will by a group of persecuted Huguenot apothecaries and their families, who believe him to be the Abbot.)

This section of Lucarotti's novelisation contains a considerably greater amount of historical trivia than the teleplay covering the same ground; much of it is relayed by a Doctor who, in this version, is intimately familiar with, for example, the building history of Notre Dame and the French state's edicts concerning apothecaries[88]. (The way the novelisation's Doctor intuits where he is in time and space using a combination of observation and historical knowledge mirrors exactly the way Barbara behaves in the opening scene of Lucarotti's *The Aztecs*, a script he had novelised shortly before.) More significantly, this enhanced knowledge of early modern France, denied to the TV serial's Doctor, means that he is aware (from p22 of a book whose main

---

[88] Pp14, 16.

narrative begins on p11) that he and Steven are in Paris a few days before a religious genocide.

This is in stark contrast to the teleplay, where he does not discover this information until p11 of 'Bell of Doom''s 29-page script[89], and his immediate instinct is to leave at that very moment (which the TARDIS does a mere eight pages later[90]). Because of this difference, the Doctor has a very different motivation for heading to see Preslin: the novelisation's Doctor heads to see Preslin specifically because he knows the Massacre is coming, whereas the TV serial's does so out of general interest in 16th-century views on germinology[91].

The novelisation's events, like the serial's, take place over four days, but Steven does not stay at either the Admiral's house or Preslin's shop overnight, or spend a whole night running from the palace guard; instead he is imprisoned on the night of the 19-20 August, and spends the night of 20-21 August in a crypt with Anne and the night of 21-22 August in the tunnels with the Huguenot refugees. (A wrinkle in the structure of the televised story may suggest that something closer to Lucarotti's final scheme underlies it. While 'War of God' explicitly takes place on 20 August 1572, the wedding of Henry of Navarre to Margaret of France is also said to have taken place 'yesterday', which would mean that the day Steven first visits the tavern is, as in the novelisation, the 19th, the wedding having taken place on the 18th.)

---

[89] A little over eight minutes into the broadcast episode.
[90] A little over seven minutes later.
[91] 'War of God'; p22 in the novelisation.

In the book, that the Doctor is not the Abbot is confirmed by Gaston and Nicholas when they come to see Preslin (whom they already know), having met the Abbot at the Louvre[92]. (Neither the Doctor nor Preslin meet Gaston or Nicholas in the serial.) Attempts are then made to persuade the Doctor to impersonate the Abbot in order to aid the Huguenots in leaving Paris. He refuses[93]. But by this time the Doctor's failure to meet Steven at the inn has led to the young man being arrested and imprisoned for a curfew violation[94]. Realising that the best way to free Steven is to impersonate the Abbot, and that he cannot in conscience impersonate the Abbot to help Steven and then refuse to do the same to help Preslin, the Doctor agrees to be part of a large-scale deception[95].

Because of this deception, Steven spends much of 20 August confused as to whether the Abbot is the Doctor or not, but by nightfall he knows that: a) there is a real Abbot and b) the Doctor is impersonating him[96]. The novelisation's Steven is therefore not as confused or alienated as his television counterpart, and he and the Doctor are reunited on the 21st and thereafter work together[97].

This is revealing of the fundamental difference in conceptions of *The Massacre* between its two authors. Discussing the serial in 1991 Tosh explained the premise as follows:

---

[92] Pp58-59.
[93] P62.
[94] Pp53-54.
[95] P63.
[96] P75.
[97] P113.

'Neither he [Steven] nor the viewer is entirely sure whether the Doctor is impersonating the Abbot or whether they are actually two different people'.[98]

This is something which is not true of the novelisation[99], where the reader always knows, and Steven quickly ascertains, that the Doctor and the Abbot are two different people. If it was also not true of Lucarotti's original scripts (a fair assumption given Lucarotti's own contention that the Doctor impersonating the Abbot is '...the basic idea of the script, with the Doctor being the double'[100]), then Tosh's comment that Lucarotti 'missed the whole point of the story' suddenly makes sense. Tosh wants a story in which it is ambiguous to the audience as to whether the Doctor and the Abbot are one person or two. Lucarotti wants a story in which the Doctor impersonates the Abbot with the full connivance of the audience. Dramatically, these intentions are irreconcilable. No wonder there was what Peter Purves has called an 'awful spat'[101] over the teleplays.

After the point roughly approximating the end of 'War of God', the novelisation and the serial almost cease to have any real

---

[98] Hearn, 'Script Editing Who, Donald Tosh'.

[99] Novelisations, of course, have readers, not viewers, but the point stands.

[100] Russell, 'Off The Shelf'. A version of the story in which the Doctor impersonates an important French official in order to secure paperwork that can release friends from captivity, so that they may escape state sponsored slaughter in the nation's capital, might be said to be clearly influenced by the earlier **Doctor Who** story *The Reign of Terror*.

[101] Adams, Matt, 'Taking the Lead'. DWM #483.

connective relationship. Beyond the setting and the characters, both of which are bequeathed by a combination of history and **Doctor Who**'s format, they are quite different from this point and grow, with the odd exceptional moment, increasingly so as they progress.

Lucarotti features a Duke of Guise, Henry of Anjou (the King's younger brother and eventual successor as Henry III) and Henry of Navarre (the brother-in-law of both Kings and the eventual successor to Henry III as Henry IV) as major characters in the scenes set in and around the court, and makes the Dukes of Guise and Anjou the key conspirators in the plot to assassinate de Coligny. He notes that Maurevert often worked for the Guises, the Guise family's personal antagonism with de Coligny and the fact that the Admiral is shot from a house belonging to the dynasty[102]. (De Teligny does not appear in the novelisation, with Gaston and Muss allowed to attend the Louvre with de Coligny.) Lucarotti does, however, make an error with regard to the Guise family. He describes the Duke of Guise of 1572 as 'Francois, Duke of Guise, the brother of the Cardinal of Lorraine. Their father, also Francois of Guise, had instigated and led the massacre at Vassy 10 years earlier' (p117). The Duke of 1572 was Henry (1550-88); Francois (1519-63) was his father. It **was** Francois who initiated Vassy, and Charles, Cardinal of Lorraine (1524-74) was **his** brother, the uncle to the Duke of 1572, not his brother. The confusion may arise from Francis himself having an uncle, Jean (1498-1550) who was himself Cardinal of Lorraine. (The hat was essentially a family possession.)

---

[102] Pp117-18.

The novelisation's description of the attempted assassination of de Coligny is drawn heavily from that in the camera script, using whole and specific phrases from the stage directions (e.g. 'a rifle of the very latest design') – something that happens nowhere else in the novelisation. The scenes featuring Bondot were part of the pre-filming for the serial, meaning these scenes would have been amongst the first shot for the story.

The idea of 'the Sea Beggar' being a codename for de Coligny does not feature in the novelisation at all, although the fact that the assassin Maurevert is codenamed 'Bondot', and the need to discover his identity, are given far greater prominence than in the scripts[103]. There are subplots about the TARDIS being taken to the Bastille as a satanic object, where the (real) Abbot attempts to exorcise it, and there is a subsequent attempt to burn it (which, naturally, fails)[104].

The reader, and eventually Steven, are encouraged to enjoy the Doctor's impersonation of the Abbot, and the licence he feels it gives him to interfere on the margins of history, as much as the Doctor himself clearly does, and the Doctor, disguised as the Abbot, is able to meet all of the story's major historical figures at least once. He attends the King's council and lectures those present on their responsibilities and, unable to resist, attempts as the Abbot to stop de Coligny's assassination – but, equally naturally, also fails[105].

In terms of plot mechanics, the marriage of Navarre to the King's sister is said to be the King's initiative and Catherine expresses

---

[103] Pp96, 99-100, 107.
[104] Pp97, 105, 111.
[105] Pp95-97, 129-31, 123.

disgust at it[106]. Catherine is aware of the plot to kill the Admiral, rather than being the motivating force behind it, thus removing the circular plot motion of 'Priest of Death'[107]; and the Massacre is, rather than the end game Catherine has had in mind all along as onscreen, a reaction to Gaston's announcement in council that he knows 'all about the conspiracy' to kill the Admiral in front of the King[108]. It is part of a cover up of Catherine's younger son's partial responsibility for the Admiral's (attempted) assassination, and Catherine's intention is to kill a few prominent figures (as onscreen Tavannes has a list of those who are to die)[109].

The novelisation's direct takings from the scripts practically end after p50. It borrows a phrase 'prevent further civil strife' from the serial's Admiral and gives it to its own[110], and there is a completely reworded but functionally identical scene in which Anne and Steven find clothes to disguise themselves[111].

Steven does still find the Abbot's corpse and initially believe it to be the Doctor's, but in this telling, he knows it's possible it's the Doctor, but is not convinced, as on television, that there is essentially no real Abbot at all[112].

The novelisation utilises a scene between Catherine and her son the King which is only lightly rewritten from that on pages 33 and

---

[106] P133. Historically, it does seem to have been Catherine's.
[107] Pp 96-97.
[108] P128.
[109] P138.
[110] 'Priest of Death'; p116 in the novelisation.
[111] Pp 81-83.
[112] Pp 126-27, 131.

34 of the 'Priest of Death' camera script[113]. Similarly, the book also uses the scene between Catherine and Tavannes from pages 14 to 16 of 'Bell of Doom' script[114]. The essential dramatic movement of the scene is the same and some of the dialogue is retained. Tavannes presents a list of certain number of Huguenots to be killed to the Queen Mother, only to be told that there will be a general slaughter instead. He ferociously argues that Navarre cannot be killed, as his death would involve France in international wars, with reprisals from Protestant countries; Catherine reluctantly concedes the point and agrees to have Navarre sent out of the city under armed guard.

The differences between these two scenes as found in the scripts and in the prose adaptation form an interesting microcosm of the differences between the novelisation and the teleplays as a whole.

In the earlier scene, Catherine mentions the Guise faction, and her younger son, whom she tells Charles would be 'ten times' the King he is. This does not happen onscreen. She also says that Navarre would usurp Charles' throne should the opportunity arise, but she does not, as onscreen, blame this on his marriage to the King's sister. At the end of the prose telling, the King breaks down and his mother calms herself and comforts him, a nuance not present in the scripts.

In the later scene, blame for ordering the Massacre is explicitly moved to the King, and it is portrayed as a spontaneous act, as

---

[113] Starting at around 19 minutes in the broadcast version of 'Priest of Death'; pp 132-33 in the novelisation.

[114] Starting at around 10 minutes in the broadcast version of 'Bell of Doom'; pp 138-39 in the novelisation.

much of a surprise to Tavannes as it is onscreen. The King, at least according to his Mother, orders the Massacre with the words 'Let no soul rest alive to reproach us'[115]. All references to Henry of Navarre are silently amended to render him a King, not a Prince.

The novelisation does not include any of the present-day material from 'Bell of Doom' (which Lucarotti considered 'clumsy'[116]) but does include a framing sequence in which the Doctor, resting in a garden, is asked by the Time Lords to account for his accounts for actions in 1572, and Dodo's arrival on the TARDIS is alluded to in that[117].

Lucarotti's book manages to contain a great deal more historical detail and anecdote (it has, in so far as such a thing is quantifiable, greater 'educational value'), while also being a version of the story in which the Doctor is the protagonist and in which his impersonation of the Abbot is key to almost all events.

So, how much, if any, of Lucarotti's 1987 telling represents his lost 1965 script? We can't know for certain. Some, maybe most of this work, both research and plotting , would have been done in the 80s, but some of it is likely to date from the original version he wrote but didn't have access to.

What **is** possible, from his comments, is to know some things that **were definitely not** in his teleplays. Lucarotti acknowledges that the tunnels under Paris, the woodcut showing the Abbot trying to

---

[115] This phrase is drawn from an anonymous account of the Massacre which purports (falsely) to be memoirs of the Duke of Anjou, later King Henry III.
[116] Russell, 'Off The Shelf'.
[117] Pp 9-10, 143-44.

stop the shooting of the Admiral and much of the historical detail about the Louvre were things he only discovered in the 1980s.

> 'I had such co-operation from the two major libraries – they just fed me one thing and another, documents, archives, everything. They were so kind and helpful, so that all I had to do when I came to write the book was to refer to an encyclopaedia for more general information. Now in one of these books, I came across an old woodcut which showed the shape of the Abbot standing in the doorway, which I then used in the book – that woodcut mentioned at the end actually exists![118] It gave me the opportunity for having the Doctor save the Admiral.'[119]

Lucarotti also indicated having the Doctor and the Abbot meet 'had to happen'[120] in the novelisation, which could be taken to mean that they did not in his script. (It would have been a technical challenge to achieve, even briefly, in 1965, and required use of the serial's film allowance. Lucarotti was very experienced in writing 'as live' videotape (VT) drama and might be unlikely to make such a demand of a production process he knew well. The novelisation contains much else that is impossible to envisage being staged in the Riverside 1 studio, with far too many scenes set outside, in and around Notre Dame cathedral and extensive sequences of the Doctor being carried around underground tunnels by dog-cart.

---

[118] I have been unable to trace this image among the near-contemporary depictions of this event, but they are so numerous a comprehensive search is almost impossible.

[119] Russell, 'Off The Shelf'.

[120] Russell, 'Off The Shelf'.

There is also no room for these in the serial's scant filming schedule, especially as these scenes would involve William Hartnell.)

It is also valid to ask what appears to have been picked out *The Massacre* in the rewrite. What is noticeable by its absence? An explanation of where the Doctor has been, and an explanation of what has happened to Preslin. These are not noticeably missing merely because they are present in the novelisation, they are lacunae in the piece as shot. A plot thread in which the Doctor explicitly enables Preslin to escape Paris before the Massacre takes place, and by posing as the Abbot, as presented in the novelisation, has almost certainly been removed by the rewrite. It is the simplest, cleanest explanation for these gaps.

Lucarotti, commenting on Tosh's scripts, has called the Doctor's non-explanation of where he has been 'unforgivable'. That's strongly judgemental, but then it was Lucarotti's work that was being amended. It is fair to say that the story as transmitted has a logical hole: the Doctor knows enough about Preslin to know his address, but not enough to know that he lived in Paris during the French Wars of Religion. More oddly, in the serial as transmitted the Doctor genuinely seems to decide to visit Preslin **before** he is certain he has arrived in Paris[121]. This kind of structural oddity is often the result of incoherent redrafting, and could be taken as internal evidence that this scene has indeed had the lines specifically concerning Preslin and the Doctor's desire to meet him amended, which would fit with our theory.

---

[121] 'War of God' camera script pages 3-5.

The serial's Doctor then (implicitly) helps Preslin to flee Paris in the few days before the Massacre, but, lacking as he does knowledge that the Massacre is about to occur, he has no reason to do so. Yes, he has established that Preslin and his fellow apothecaries are oppressed in France, but how would sending him out of the city help that? In any case, the Preslin of the teleplay is not, unlike that of the novelisation, explicitly a Huguenot.

Donald Tosh has said that 'equally the more that is known about a certain period of history, the more restrictive it becomes on your regular characters'[122]. Is this why the teleplay's Doctor shows an ignorance of history at variance with his usual portrayal, and one which causes logical problems with regard to his actions with Preslin? And is this, in part, why the more plausibly ignorant Steven becomes the serial's protagonist for more than half its length?

Conjecturally then, we can propose a rough, hypothetical shape for Lucarotti's version of *The Massacre* for television, drawing on all the available evidence.

A first episode largely like that transmitted, but one in which, as in the novelisation, the Doctor's resemblance to the Abbot is a point of discussion between him and Preslin in their scenes together and in which he agrees to impersonate the Abbot as part of a plan to get Preslin (and possibly other apothecaries) out of France. In this version, again as in the novelisation, the Doctor has a broader knowledge of the period and is aware there is a state-sponsored mass killing on the horizon. The apothecaries are hiding out

---

[122] Stevens, 'Donald Tosh Interview'.

inPreslin's shop, not the catacombs of Paris. The episode still ends with the revelation of the Abbot's face.

The second episode is less circular, with its exact content depending on whether or not Hartnell was originally anticipated as attending the recording of the episode or not. Certainly, given its verifiable source in historical anecdote, the Doctor impersonates the Abbot, possibly off-screen.

It is the discovery that Bondot is Maurevert that motivates the action, not that de Coligny is 'The Sea Beggar'. The transmitted episode has two conflicting subplots about codenames, one of which is given massive emphasis, one of which is thrown away. I conjecture that the latter, the one retained in the novelisation, and which has a historical basis, is the original. Internal evidence can again be seen to support this position. Anne and Steven's final scene in 'The Sea Beggar' is a film sequence. This, shot first as it was, might be spared rewriting if time was short. While the subplot about de Colingy's codename is referenced in this it is done so inelegantly and briefly. (The square brackets below are mine.)

STEVEN

Anne, what are you doing following me?

ANNE

I'm sorry, Monsieur, I didn't mean any harm.

STEVEN

What are you doing here? The curfew's ringing. Go back to the house.

ANNE

No. I can't go back there now. They'll know where to find me. I want to come with you.

STEVEN

But you can't, I mean, and why?

ANNE

You were kind to me. You're the first one that ever was. Please, don't send me back there.

STEVEN

I can't take you with me. I've nowhere to go myself.

ANNE

Well, I know Paris, I'll help you find somewhere.

STEVEN

[Well, I...

HE HAS A SUDDEN THOUGHT

Do you know who the Seabeggar is?

ANNE

What?

STEVEN

Who is the Seabeggar?

ANNE

I don't know, Monsieur. Why?

STEVEN

He will be killed tomorrow....] All right if you insist on coming with me, do you know where we can spend tonight?

ANNE

We can't go to my Aunt's – they will be looking for me there. But there must be lots of places in Paris where no one would think of finding me.

STEVEN

Of course, Preslin's shop! Do you know how to get to the Port Saint Martin?

ANNE

Of course.

STEVEN

Take me there. I've only been there once and I doubt if I could find my way at night

ANNE (DELIGHTED)

Of course, monsieur. I'll show you.

Steven and Anne talk about their present situation, divert into Steven's worries about 'the seabeggar' (as it is rendered in the script) via a non-sequitur and then return to the original topic of the scene after some clumsy ellipses. If the material I have placed in brackets is removed, the scene is neater and more coherent. The discussion of 'the seabeggar' sits sufficiently ill in it that it is hard not to conclude that it is an interpolation into an already-written discussion.

In our hypothetical second episode Steven, as in the transmitted version, is kept away from the Doctor, but does catch sight of someone who may be either the Abbot or the Doctor, but believes him to be the latter. (Perhaps the real Abbot appears only on film, as in the transmitted episode, allowing Hartnell, if in studio, to play the Doctor and the Doctor impersonating the Abbot only.) Roger Colbert is a smaller character, or does not feature at all.

In the third episode, there is a larger role for Hartnell, who features as both the Doctor and the Abbot, the former impersonating the latter, and arranging the paperwork for the apothecaries' exit from Paris, as in the novelisation. (In the transmitted episode Hartnell's two scenes together run for less than five minutes. That's not Hartnell's screen time or speaking time. That's the total length of the scenes he's in.) The Doctor and Steven are reunited. The Doctor attends the King's council as the Abbot. Possibly the TARDIS is taken to the Bastille as in the book. Anne is captured by the Abbot's men. (On screen, they simply stop looking for her, without acknowledgement, in between 'The Sea Beggar' and 'Priest of Death': another vanishing subplot.) The Doctor almost certainly meets Catherine de Medici while 'in character' as the Abbot. (Wiles and Tosh would hardly have debated, as per their own comments, whether the Doctor should do this or not if the idea had never been considered, and the scene in which the Doctor encounters the Queen is one of the best in the book: this is a situation which, of course, also puts a different light on Tosh's statement of the need 'not to show people like Catherine de Medici doing things they didn't do'[123].)

---

[123] Hearn, 'Script Editing Who, Donald Tosh'.

The final episode stages the assassination attempt on de Coligny. The Doctor continues to impersonate the Abbot, this time in order to free Anne. One of the Abbots is murdered by Duval. Steven, and possibly the audience, is unsure which. The Doctor and Steven reunite at the TARDIS, and the Doctor tells Steven that de Coligny and his friends cannot be saved. They depart in the TARDIS with a new passenger: Anne Chaplet.

> 'Annette Robertson was a lovely girl. It was mooted that she was going to take over [as a regular companion] but I wasn't party to any of the discussions about it.'[124]

> [Peter Purves]

> 'Instead of having Anne as the companion [as planned] we introduced Dodo who had the same surname as Anne and whose grandmother was French.'[125]

> [Donald Tosh]

> 'John Wiles was an idiot... Just look at what happened during the time I was there: five girls, total confusion as far as writers were concerned about what was going on.'[126]

> [Peter Purves]

The Massacre 's producer, John Wiles, was only **Doctor Who**'s second; he had taken over from Verity Lambert, who had worked on the series since its inception, and played a significant role in its creation, at the very end of the second production block. Wiles

---

[124] Adams, 'Taking the Lead'.
[125] Hearn, 'Script Editing Who, Donald Tosh'.
[126] Adams, 'Taking the Lead'.

arrived and departed inside nine months; and ended up being credited on only 24 episodes, 12 of which formed a Dalek serial that he didn't want to make and later said he had washed his hands of.[127]

His Story Editor, Donald Tosh, with whom he was in creative and personal sympathy and with whom he had a pre-existing friendship, arrived around a month before Wiles did and resigned in solidarity when Wiles handed in his own notice, although availability of replacements ultimately meant Wiles stayed in post a few weeks longer than Tosh did, despite resigning first. (Tosh was credited on 29 episodes, one as a freelance author.)

During this period, the series' viewing figures collapsed (albeit for reasons that are still not easily understood – see Appendix 5, 'Reception and Ratings') , and the series went through four (or five) female leads, at least one of whom was informed her services were no longer required at less than a month's notice.

Maureen O'Brien's contract was originally due to expire with the fourth episode of the third production block[128], scheduled to be shot in early October, but on 20 July 1965 the BBC added a 20-episode extension option to that contract, and there was an expectation on both sides that it would be taken up. (Indeed, Terry Nation's storyline for *The Daleks' Master Plan,* still extant, features Vicki throughout.)

---

[127] Bentham, 'John Wiles Interview'.
[128] Ultimately 'Horse of Destruction' (*The Myth Makers* episode 4, 1965).

On 3 September 1965, after returning from a pre-season holiday, O'Brien was informed that the BBC had decided not to take up this option after all. This was between location shooting for *The Myth Makers* and the recording for its first episode, i.e. the first episode of the third production block, giving O'Brien three weeks' notice that she was no longer required on **Doctor Who**.

Donald Tosh has often indicated that Wiles was unhappy with comments O'Brien made about the scripts for *Galaxy 4* (1965), produced during the handover between Lambert and Wiles. In light of this, it is hard not to interpret his sudden decision to reverse O'Brien's formally agreed contract extension as a fit of pique. Interviewed in 1981, Wiles would indicate that it was O'Brien's decision to leave, and that her departure was arranged before he became producer[129]; an account that does not accord with the production paperwork or the recollections of anyone else involved. It certainly ushered in a period of instability over **Doctor Who**'s female lead that wouldn't quite be resolved until after Wiles' own departure.

> 'Maureen didn't know she was being written out, that was a big shock, and then there was Adrienne Hill for four episodes, and then there was Jean Marsh.'[130]
>
> [Peter Purves]

The initial choice to replace Vicki was Katarina, a Trojan handmaiden who was introduced in the same episode in which

---

[129] McLachlan, Ian, 'The John Wiles Interview Part 1', *TARDIS* vol 6 #1, 1981.
[130] Adams, 'Taking the Lead'.

Vicki made her final appearance. She would be written out within five episodes, dying in 'The Traitors' (*The Daleks' Master Plan* episode 4, 1965).

> '... with regard to Katarina, I realised the character we had created wasn't going to work when I started reading Paul Erickson's early scripts for *The Ark* [1966], and it was very clear what the problem was. Everything had to be explained to this girl. And I mean, absolutely everything, because she came from a primitive and distant past and was being transported to a far distant future. And I said, "We can't do this! Every story will be dragged down again and again to make room for explanations."'[131]

> [Donald Tosh]

The decision that Katarina would not be retained for long was made so quickly that, despite the production team's initial intention to keep her on permanently (one that was, by Tosh's account, communicated to freelancers writing serials for later in the year), Adrienne Hill shot her death scene, which formed part of *The Daleks' Master Plan*'s pre-filming, before any others as the character.

Sara Kingdom, a character from the future who featured in *The Daleks' Master Plan* from its fifth episode onwards, did not continue when Jean Marsh made clear that she wasn't interested in staying in **Doctor Who** beyond one story. It may also be relevant that the character was created by Terry Nation, who later used her in other projects. Nation was always effective in protecting his

---

[131] Hearn, 'Script Editing Who, Donald Tosh'.

ownership of intellectual property and it is impossible to imagine him allowing the character to be used without payment being made for her appearances.

According to Tosh, it was quickly ascertained that Anne, as a regular character, created many of the same problems as Katarina, requiring vast amounts of information to be exposited to her in order to plausibly function in science-fiction adventure stories. He has also indicated that there was a concern that taking Anne from the 1570s would constitute interference in history.

> 'That was why at the end of *The Massacre* the Doctor was unable to save Anne Chaplet, the French servant girl, by taking her with them even though it seemed a very hard decision to make.'[132]

> [Donald Tosh]

This suggests an extremely abstract concept of the notion of 'changing' history, where even a minor change to an unrecorded event (e.g. taking a wholly unknown French peasant woman away from her own time and place) can be seen to potentially have a devastating effect on the future. Tosh has indicated[133] the influence of Ray Bradbury's 'A Sound of Thunder' (1952) on his thinking in this regard. Incoming producer Innes Lloyd would later echo this with his observation that while the series could effectively do stories using 'historical backgrounds [...] we will not involve Doctor

---

[132] Hearn, 'Script Editing Who, Donald Tosh'.
[133] Hearn, Marcus, 'Script Editing Who, Donald Tosh', DWM #192. (This is part 2 of the interview begun in DWM #191.)

Who and his companions in events which cannot be changed because they really happened.'[134]

We can reasonably surmise that the relatively late decision to not take Anne on board at the end of the story is another root cause of the rewrites, and not just because more than a third of 'Bell of Doom''s length is devoted to introducing a replacement character. In a story where Anne joins the TARDIS crew, the Doctor wouldn't use 'not changing the course of history' as an excuse to leave her behind, possibly to die, and therefore there is no possibility of this conflicting with his just having spent three episodes saving Preslin. But if Anne must be sent away so as to not change history, the removal of the plot thread in which the Doctor overtly arranges Preslin's flight from Paris becomes necessary, because the Doctor cannot be seen to save Preslin[135] but abandon Anne without this causing too much of a contradiction. There really is nothing else that he can be doing for the bulk of the story, but this is not acknowledged except obliquely, presumably for fear of drawing attention to this. The novelisation resolves this paradox by sending Anne and her family to Picardy, with their journey there protected by documents given to them by the Doctor which carry the authority of the Abbot of Amboise. As noted above, and as the Doctor tells Steven after Anne has left, in Picardy the state actively sought to protect the Huguenot minority as the nationwide Massacre began. (What the Doctor does not note, however, is that the Governor of Picardy, while a Catholic, had been raised as a

---

[134] Howe, David, Mark Stammers and Stephen James Walker, *Doctor Who: The Handbook – The Second Doctor*, p 123.
[135] Or perhaps, just perhaps, Pierre Touillet.

Huguenot before converting in adulthood, and his mother was still of the 'Reformists'. As good a microcosm as anyone could wish for to demonstrate how personal interaction with, and knowledge of, other cultures prevents the kind of 'othering' of minorities that the serial demonstrates.)

The identity of the series' female lead was not, however, even the biggest casting-related issue facing the **Doctor Who** office during this serial's active production.

> '[Wiles] tried very hard to get rid of Bill. "How can we lose him?" That was John Wiles. But [BBC Head of Serials] Gerald Savory said "No, not under any circumstances".'[136]
>
> [Peter Purves]

When John Wiles took over from Verity Lambert, William Hartnell had a contract that took him through to the 28th episode of the series' third production block. This episode was ultimately 'The Final Test' (*The Celestial Toymaker* episode 4, 1966). It was Wiles' intention that this serial (another story heavily rewritten by Donald Tosh[137] in which Steven Taylor/Peter Purves takes the lead in the

---

[136] Adams, 'Taking the Lead'.

[137] It was then rewritten once again by Gerry Davis after Tosh's departure. Tosh had included the eponymous characters George and Margaret from the 1937 West End hit play of that title written BBC Head of Serials Gerald Savory. George and Margaret are offstage characters in Savory's play, whose arrival the onstage characters anticipate with dread. Savory objected to their finally arriving in an unconnected work, forcing Davis to undertake a substantial redraft to remove them. *George and Margaret* was, and is, still in copyright and has been adapted for the screen half a

middle two instalments) should be Hartnell's final **Doctor Who**. In the story as transmitted, the Doctor is rendered invisible by the Toymaker for the middle two episodes (and indeed much of the first). Wiles intended that when the Doctor was restored to visibility in 'The Final Test' and he returned to his friends, he would be played by a different actor.

Obviously, this did not happen. Hartnell's contract was renewed up to the end of the third recording block in early February 1966, during recording of *The Massacre*. By this time, Wiles was being trailed by his successor as producer, Innes Lloyd, and the paperwork indicates Lloyd's responsibility for this renewal (although Tosh has said that Hartnell's contract was renewed in error[138] by BBC administrators).

While **Doctor Who**'s regular cast was entitled to weeks away from the series, in recognition of the sheer number of episodes made each year on a weekly schedule, the minimisation of Hartnell's contributions to **Doctor Who** towards the end of Wiles' brief producership is striking. The 14 episodes from 'The Abandoned Planet' to 'The Final Test' are particularly noticeable in their general eschewing of Hartnell's involvement, something that emerges into even sharper perspective in light of Hartnell's contract situation. Hartnell appears only in (some of) a pre-filmed 18-second insert in 'The Sea Beggar', and in only two scenes in 'Priest of Death'; he also has a minimal role in 'The Abandoned Planet', is largely present only through pre-filming for 'The Destruction of Time', is absent

---

dozen times. (*The Celestial Toymaker*'s original author, Brian Hayles, receives the only onscreen writing credit for the serial.)
[138] Hearn, 'Script Editing Who, Donald Tosh'.

from (the Lloyd-produced but Wiles-planned) 'The Dancing Floor' (*The Celestial Toymaker* episode 3, 1966) and features only in pre-recorded voiceover in 'The Hall of Dolls' (*The Celestial Toymaker* episode 2, 1966), and his entrances are delayed and involvement restricted in both 'Bell of Doom' and 'The Final Test'.

When asked about this Donald Tosh has simply said:

> 'At a guess, I'd say that Bill just wanted some time off, and it was as simple as that. We were very aware that it was a punishing schedule and we had to give the man a certain amount of time off every now and again... Either he had asked for it, or **we felt he needed it**.'[139]

The effective promotion of Peter Purves to co-lead for *The Massacre* and *The Celestial Toymaker* has been described by Donald Tosh thus: 'Both John Wiles and myself felt that Peter as Steven was underused. The character is an obvious identification figure for our young male audience; after all, few nine to twelve year old small boys are going to identify with the Doctor as played by Bill.'[140]

In light of all this, it is very hard to not conclude that Hartnell's contributions were being minimised in the run-up to his anticipated departure. This was perhaps as an attempt to acclimatise **Doctor Who**'s audience to the idea of the series without him. It could equally simply have been the case that Wiles shared Tosh's view on

---

[139] Stevens, 'Donald Tosh Interview'. The emphasis here is mine.
[140] Stevens, 'Donald Tosh Interview'.

the appeal, or lack of, of Hartnell's Doctor[141]. It may have been as banal as a personality clash between Hartnell and Wiles, with no deeper underlying reason.

'As for Bill and John Wiles, well, I was piggy in the middle, but as the director you often were.'[142]

[Paddy Russell]

Whatever the root cause, Wiles' actions in relation to O'Brien's contract – despite the problems it created for the rest of his period in charge – indicate a methodology of making structural changes in response to challenges to his authority as **Doctor Who**'s new producer without looking at potential consequences.

'The feeling from above was that the show works now, and will continue to run as long as Bill Hartnell plays the Doctor. So perhaps I was mad for wanting to change it.'[143]

[John Wiles]

Tosh's comments about Hartnell's Doctor stand in stark contrast to Verity Lambert's feelings about and professed faith in Hartnell's

---

[141] Hartnell's ostensible ill health is frequently quoted in relation to this period, but there is little evidence of this onscreen in the stories made immediately after Wiles' departure, e.g. *The Gunfighters*, *The War Machines* and even the first two extant episodes of *The Tenth Planet* (1966), nor the recently discovered filmed interview conducted with Hartnell shortly after his departure from **Doctor Who**.

[142] Marson, 'Paddy's Field!'.

[143] Bentham, 'John Wiles Interview'.

portrayal's appeal to children[144], and frankly don't bear scrutiny. **Doctor Who**, starring Hartnell, had been an enormous success in 1964 and 1965, with colossal viewing figures including episodes which were among the top 10 most watched programmes the week they were transmitted, and a positive public response, especially from children. He made extensive appearances in character, including very many at children's hospitals, and dealt with a huge postbag of fan mail which, again, was dominated by letters from children[145].

Peter Purves is no doubt as to who to blame for these issues:

> 'John Wiles resigned... because he'd got wind of the fact that he was going to be sacked, which he should have been. He was totally incompetent. He wasn't a very nice man – I had no rapport with him, I didn't respect him, I didn't think he knew what he was doing... all the reasons why you would dislike someone who was actually senior to you, but you knew couldn't do the job. He was stupid.'[146]

(Incidental evidence of Wiles' anecdotal, alleged incompetence is found in how the pre-filming for 'Bell of Doom' and the studio

---

[144] See, for example, *More Than Thirty Years in the TARDIS*, 6m to 9m.

[145] If the argument is that **Doctor Who** would have been more successful starring someone else other than Hartnell, then leaving aside the unprovable nature of the hypothesis, it is worth noting that by many measures it has never been quite as successful as it was during 1964-65 at any point in the following 50 years, regardless of who played the lead.

[146] Adams, 'Taking the Lead'.

recording for 'The Abandoned Planet' were scheduled for the same day (7 February) when both required the series' sole TARDIS prop. Photographs taken on location show a hastily assembled and rough TARDIS not seen in the series before or since. It is also notable that **Doctor Who** began its third transmitted 'series' with five episodes in hand, but by January 1966 was recording less than a fortnight ahead of transmission. In interviews Wiles said he had resigned the producership of **Doctor Who** in order to safeguard his own mental health, and that he was unhappy as, and unsuited to, being a producer.)

> 'I knew I had added nothing of any worth to the programme and I would never get anywhere with it but a total blank. I couldn't win against Bill. Perhaps I didn't deserve to. I didn't want the job.'[147]

[John Wiles]

It's worth considering the fact that John Wiles thought it even possible, let alone advisable, to replace Hartnell as the star of **Doctor Who**, even if he was prevented from doing so by BBC management. The concept of 'regeneration', of replacing the lead actor of **Doctor Who** through showing the character undergo an onscreen metamorphosis is usually perceived as a brilliant, unexpected piece of improvisation by the production team of Innes Lloyd and Gerry Davis when faced with William Hartnell's declining health. But that Wiles and Tosh were actively pursuing a similar action a year earlier must change our perspective on Hartnell's

---

[147] McLachlan, Ian, 'The John Wiles Interview Part 2', TARDIS vol 6 #2, 1981.

eventual departure. (In 2014 Tosh would go so far as to effectively claim to be the creator of the concept of regeneration and to have 'left behind the idea' for his successors [148].)

One plausible influence on Wiles' thinking is that, between the showings of 'Checkmate' (*The Time Meddler* episode 4, 1965) on 24 July and 'Four Hundred Dawns' (*Galaxy 4* episode 1, 1965) on 11 September 1965, and between the recordings of *Mission to the Unknown* (1965) (6 August) and 'Temple of Secrets' (17 September), in the exact period when Wiles was formally taking over the producership of **Doctor Who,** the feature film *Dr Who and the Daleks* (Gordon Flemyng, 1965) was released. In this, as anyone reading this is almost certainly aware, the lead character was played not by William Hartnell but by Peter Cushing. This was in part a matter of scheduling (the film had been shot during the recording of the second series) and in part because Cushing was, in

---

[148] Smith, 'Doctor Who story editor Donald Tosh'. This is rather odd on several levels, as 'regeneration' as it is now understood by the wider audience is not really invented until 1974, when the term is coined and the idea of when the actor playing the Doctor being a natural process, a response to injury or illness, is introduced and retrospectively applied to the recastings of *The Tenth Planet* / *The Power of the Daleks* (1966) and *The War Games* (1969) / *Spearhead from Space* (1970). Textually in the first instance, the Doctor claims he's 'been renewed' and that 'it's part of the TARDIS; without it I couldn't survive!', while publicity for the series implied the Doctor had simply been reduced in physical age, i.e. that what Troughton was playing was Hartnell's character had been like as a younger man. The implication of *The War Games* is that the Doctor's appearance will be altered so as to prevent embarrassment and confusion for him on Earth.

a way Hartnell was not, a recognisable film star as far as the American market was concerned.

From this specific point in the series' history, someone else had played the leading role in **Doctor Who**. Before this, the part was wholly associated with William Hartnell. More, the film was an enormous financial, and a modest critical, success. No one could say that Cushing had failed. (Dalek creator Terry Nation would later recall that the film made so much money so quickly that the producers were unable to hide the profits quickly enough to prevent him receiving the 'piece' of it he was due[149], which he regarded as par for the course when it came to the motion picture business).

The success of the Cushing-led film did not make the replacement of Hartnell inevitable, but it made it conceivable. It may be that the simple fact that it had happened made it possible for Wiles to imagine making **Doctor Who** for television without Hartnell. It may also be that there being another actor associated with 'his' part and in the more 'permanent' medium of cinema (and a second film and a radio series, the latter of which never materialised, were quickly announced) was a factor in Hartnell's unhappiness over this period. It certainly meant that the idea of replacing him had a meaning it would not had had a year earlier. This, as much as a family bereavement he suffered during recording of *The Myth Makers* and the sudden absence of familiar and supportive figures both in front of and behind the camera, could be a contributing factor towards the difficulties faced, or indeed created, by the actor during this period.

---

[149] *Dalekmania*, 47m.

Whatever the deeper causes of the problems within the series were, Wiles' successor Innes Lloyd clearly concurred with some of his analysis regarding **Doctor Who**'s future. He very quickly removed and replaced the entire regular cast of **Doctor Who**, including Hartnell, although he went about it both more delicately and far more successfully than Wiles had done.

It may well be that the real reason for both producers wanting Hartnell to leave **Doctor Who** as soon as it could be arranged was simply that his salary of around £350 per episode was extremely high for the star of weekly VT drama series (Equity minimum for a speaking role in a TV drama production had been £9.9s as recently as 1961). Patrick Troughton would start his **Doctor Who** career earning significantly less.

Peter Purves' contract ended with 'The Bomb', the final episode of *The Ark*. Between the recording of the first and second episodes of that serial he was offered a contract for an additional 12 episodes beyond its end, it being made clear at this point that the last episode of this new contract would see Steven/Purves leave the series. This was during Lloyd's first week officially in charge of **Doctor Who**, the last of February 1966. Lane's original contract (dated 29 December 1965) was for 13 episodes. An additional six episodes were appended to this on 26 April 1966, the week Lane recorded the 11th episode of her original contract. Hartnell's contract had been extended to the end of the third production block early in Lloyd's tenure; Lloyd extended it again to cover an additional serial at the beginning of the fourth production block but no further. This effectively gave Hartnell, like Purves, three months' notice that he was leaving **Doctor Who**. Lane had two months' notice of the end of job she'd been in for under three, compared to

O'Brien's being given three weeks' notice of the end of a job she'd been in for over a year. (The recent discovery of a draft of *The Tenth Planet* episode 4 (1966), Hartnell's last episode of **Doctor Who**, which does not include a scene in which the Doctor is 'renewed' but instead a coda in which the Doctor, Ben and Polly go merrily on their way after defeating the Cybermen may prompt some reassessment of the exact speed and order of events in this later period.)

Lloyd's replacement companions, Ben and Polly, would be with the series for a year, while his selection of Patrick Troughton as Hartnell's successor is arguably **the** key event in turning **Doctor Who** into a programme capable of constant renewal, and thus potentially limitless continuation: Troughton's decision to play the part in his own way, almost without reference to Hartnell's performance and certainly outwith the grandfather archetype Hartnell's characterisation often referenced, effectively granted permission to his (potential) successors to do the same, whereas Cushing's performance, whatever its merits, was clearly, while not an imitation of Hartnell's, certainly within the same vein.

It seems, then, that we have several potentially destructive issues intersecting during the writing and production of this serial. There is a profound disagreement between Lucarotti and Tosh over the essential point of the serial, and further disagreements between them over historical interpretation (It is genuinely impossible to say which of the two men's interpretation of these events is more 'accurate'.) There is an attested confrontation between the series' new producer and established star, which takes the form of the minimisation of the star's contributions to the series over a four-month period that would, had the producer won, have led to

Hartnell's departure from **Doctor Who** offscreen and mid-serial. This is perhaps a result of, or maybe a contributing factor to, said star's oft-noted declining health. There is also an additional issue around the female lead of the series which likewise continues for months.

Frankly, the serial should be some kind of disaster. In so far as we can tell, and without actually having a copy of it, it very obviously isn't. Why is that? For Peter Purves, 'The end result' of the rewriting 'was a fantastic script – an absolutely superb script'[150], and it is hard to deny that the scripts that were shot are thematically complex and layered, with a lot of very good dialogue. There are plotting issues, but many of these feed, either by accident or design, into the serial's themes, and what may be accidental ambiguities and unresolved issues compliment the intentional ones in ways that are to the drama's ultimate benefit.

The serial also has a quality cast, who wring every ounce of dramatic ambiguity, subtext, character complexity and moral weight out of the scripts. Purves, who is himself superb throughout, has noted that 'This was a time when actors were suddenly realising that television might be a medium to work in, as opposed to it just being something you watched and theatre being a place you worked,' but that is not the whole of it. Much credit must also go to Paddy (Patricia) Russell, the serial's director.

Russell, one of the first two women to qualify from the BBC internal director's course, had been an assistant to Rudolph Cartier, one of the great pioneers of British television studio drama, and had

---

[150] Adams, 'Taking the Lead'.

worked with him on such ground-breaking productions as the first three **Quatermass** serials (1953-59) and *Doctor Korczak and the Children* (1962). The cast she assembled for *The Massacre* reflects the contacts of someone with considerable experience in television, despite being a relatively new director, as well as her abilities as an actors' director. In some ways it is more like a 21st-century **Doctor Who** story, in that nearly every member of the speaking cast has a profile of their own.

David Weston (Nicholas) has been prominent in the National Theatre, Royal Shakespeare Company and Old Vic Companies and founded the National Youth Theatre. Eric Thompson (Gaston) is best known for having voiced **The Magic Roundabout** and being the father of Emma Thompson (and husband of Phyllida Law), but as a theatre director he worked extensively with Alan Ayckbourn at that writer's peak, and as an actor was a stalwart of the Old Vic in the 1950s. André Morrell (Tavannes) was one of the earliest star actors of British television, and often worked for Cartier, including as Quatermass himself. Leonard Sachs was the star/host of the long running **The Good Old Days**. The little-known Barry Justice makes something distinctive, complex and human out of the King, who only appears in a single episode, playing him as an easily-bored hysteric afraid of his own mind, who is still somehow sympathetic. (Justice, who often worked for Russell, and who is also very memorable in ITV's adaptation of Noel Coward's *The Vortex* (1969) and *The Pallisers* (1974), was born in British India in the same city as Waris Hussein, **Doctor Who**'s first director. He is the subject of several photographic studies by Francis Goodman that are in the collection of the National Gallery of Great Britain.)

It is these actors' performances, alongside Purves and Hartnell, which enable **Doctor Who**, a tea-time adventure series about a time-travelling wizard and his friends, to negotiate its way through an event of extraordinary historical complexity and almost unmatchable human horror without seeming crass.

If the duplicate Doctor-Abbots present in both versions of *The Massacre* echo the two different paths to God offered by Catholicism and Calvinism, then perhaps *The Massacre*'s two authors – with their distinct and incompatible versions of that story, the events it portrays and the circumstances surrounding its drafting and production – can also represent alternative conceptions of God: the two-faced Doctor-Abbots simultaneously pulling anyone engaging with the serial and the novel, let alone their writing and production, in opposing directions.

This is odd to experience and, unless Lucarotti's original drafts were to turn up, can never be satisfactorily resolved – and even then only with regard to the drafting of the serial, not its production or the office politics surrounding either process.

Fortunately the contradictions surrounding *The Massacre* can, like the contradictions surrounding the Massacre, if interrogated, hopefully enhance our understanding. As to which is 'better', which provides the more accurate portrayal of Saint-Bartholomew or which more properly represents the agreed-upon collective intention of **Doctor Who**'s production and writing team when they set out to make Serial W, assuming that there ever was such a thing?

Let's leave that as a matter for the individual conscience.

APPENDIX 1: PRODUCTION TIMELINE

Dates are taken from BBC documentation. Details of other stories in active production while *The Massacre* was being shot are included in order to give a fuller idea of the schedule on which **Doctor Who** was produced.

Thursday 24 June 1965

John Lucarotti's Erik the Red storyline formally rejected.

Tuesday 6 July 1965

Untitled serial commissioned from Lucarotti.

Tuesday 20 July 1965

Four first draft scripts accepted as *The War of God*.

Friday 8 October 1965

Second draft of 'Bell of Doom' submitted.

Monday 3 January 1966

Ealing filming:

>   *Anne being chased by guards.* ('War of God' Telecine 2.)

Tuesday 4 January 1966

Ealing filming:

>   *Assassination attempt on de Coligny.* ('Priest of Death' T/C 2.)

Dead faces (Close ups of de Coligny, de Teligny, Muss). ('Bell of Doom' T/C 2.)

Wednesday 5 January 1966

Ealing filming:

Nicholas running through the streets. ('Priest of Death' T/C 3 and 5.)

Anne following Steven. ('The Sea Beggar' T/C 8.)

Thursday 6 January 1966

Ealing filming:

Exterior establishing shot of de Coligny's house. ('The Sea Beggar' T/C 3 and 4.)

Abbot outside de Coligny's house. ('The Sea Beggar' T/C 2.)

Steven at the Abbot's house. ('The Sea Beggar' T/C 4 to 8.)

Friday 7 January 1966

Wimbledon Common filming:

Dodo arriving at the TARDIS. ('Bell of Doom' T/C 3.)

TARDIS dematerialising. ('Bell of Doom' T/C 4.)

'The Abandoned Planet' recorded (20:30 to 21:45, BBC Television Centre, Studio 3).

Friday 14 January 1966

'The Destruction of Time' recorded (20:30 to 21:45, BBC Television Centre, Studio 3).

Friday 21 January 1966

'War of God' recorded (20:30 to 21:45, Riverside Studios, Stage 1).

Monday 24 January 1966

Ealing filming:

    ('The Steel Sky' (*The Ark* episode 1) T/C).

Friday 28 January 1966

'The Sea Beggar' recorded (20:30 – 21:45, Riverside Studios, Stage 1).

Friday 4 February 1966

'Priest of Death' recorded (20:30 – 21:45, Riverside Studios, Stage 1).

Saturday 5 February 1966

'War of God' transmitted.

Friday 11 February 1966

'Bell of Doom' recorded (20:30 – 21:45, Riverside Studios, Stage 1).

Saturday 12 February 1966

'The Sea Beggar' transmitted.

Friday 18 February 1966

'The Steel Sky' recorded (20:30 – 21:45, Riverside Studios, Stage 1).

Saturday 19 February 1966

'Priest of Death' transmitted.

Friday 15 February 1966

'The Plague' (*The Ark* episode 2) recorded (20:30 – 21:45, Riverside Studios, Stage 1).

Saturday 26 February 1966

'Bell of Doom' transmitted.

APPENDIX 2: FLIGHT OF THE DODO

The assumption that the final scenes of 'Bell of Doom' have little to do with those that precede it has, I hope, been interrogated in the preceding pages. However, they are in some ways set apart from them, being told largely from the point of view of a character who has not appeared in the first four-fifths of the episode, let alone the previous three instalments, and who knows nothing of what transpired therein. For that reason alone, any discussion of the character of Dorothea 'Dodo' Chaplet, while necessary if one is to fully engage with *The Massacre*, is going to be at a slight remove from that of the rest of the serial. (This, in case you haven't realised it, is my excuse for dealing with the character in an appendix.)

Dodo is an oddity. She appears in 19 episodes of **Doctor Who** transmitted across exactly as many weeks, and which between them span six serials. She only appears in the final episode of her first serial and the first two episodes of her final serial, arriving in a coda and exiting in a hurry. She is not even given the dignity of being written out onscreen. Instead a message is conveyed from the character via her replacement, Polly, and on receiving it the Doctor seems more irritated by her rudeness than sad to see her go.

The briefness of Dodo's tenure, then, means that the character remains ill-defined both within the fiction and within **Doctor Who** related discourse. There is an additional reason for this, and it's paradoxical. The arbitrary nature of archive survival for the **Doctor Who** of 1966-67 means that more than half of Lane's episodes, 11 in total, exist. More importantly, she features in three completely extant stories. This means that, when monochrome began to be available to PBS stations in America (and thus to the fan VHS black market in the UK) and later when it was shown on UK Gold, fans had three whole serials featuring the character to paw over.(This was in the days before there were known to be high-quality audio recordings of all missing episodes in existence. Naturally, these allow a fuller, although not complete, understanding of the episodes.) Our access to **Doctor Who**'s past remains partial, but it was more so then. With Dodo, the unimportant girl, we felt we had enough material to bargain out a collective judgement. Three whole stories? More than half her episodes? Plenty to puzzle over, digest, and base judgements on.

Compare this with Ben and Polly, who appeared for far longer (37 episodes each) but who are represented by a handful (nine) of what it seems we must now call 'orphan' episodes and who only feature in a single complete story – one which they share with Dodo.

This means their exposure was, and to a lesser extent remains, limited.

The upshot of this is we thought we knew Dodo, when we don't; while we accepted that we don't really know much of Ben and Polly. Even now, with every adventure featuring all three of them available on CD, we don't know the characters as well as we could. The recovery of a copy of the previously missing 'Air Lock' (*Galaxy 4* episode 3, 1965) in 2011 demonstrated beautifully that you could be someone who'd listened to a **Doctor Who** episode ad nauseam and still have a film print of the episode be a revelation.

There is, incidentally, something delightful about how closely this situation mirrors the position we find ourselves in with regard to the flightless extinct bird from which Dorothea's nickname is taken. No complete dodo specimens exist. Not one. And its extinction wasn't noted for centuries after it must have occurred. Virtually everything we know about the bird is conjectural, based on partial evidence, yet accepted widely by people who haven't ever looked at it, entirely fairly assuming those who have: a) are certain and b) have good reasons to be so. Neither of which is the case.

So, what **do** we know about Dodo? We first see her in the mid-1960s. In *The War Machines* (1966) she is surprised that the Post Office Tower 'is finished'. As the structure was completed in 15 July 1964 and it was opened in 8 October 1965, this dialogue may suggest her first scene in 'Bell of Doom' is set before one or both of these dates. What else? She explicitly tells Steven that both her parents are dead, and in 'The Celestial Toyroom' (*The Celestial Toymaker* episode 1, 1966), there is a flashback to her 'on the day my mother died'. The script indicates that the past Dodo should be in school uniform for this scene. With the episode non-extant and no photographs from the sequence available it is impossible to tell if the past Dodo being of school age is meant to confirm that the present Dodo is too, or explicitly rule it out. (Is Lane made up and hair styled to be younger in the flashback, or does she retain her look from the 'present' sequences? We just don't know.)

The Doctor refers to Dodo as 'child' but then he does this to Polly, who is explicitly written as an independent, employed adult woman (she is 'twenty four' according to the writers guide issued in June 1966) and indeed to Sara Kingdom, played by the then 31-year-old Jean Marsh. The Doctor also draws attention to a perceived

136

resemblance between Dodo and Susan[151], coding her as being, like Vicki, a substitute granddaughter for him. The first thing Steven says to Dodo is to ask her about her parents, suggesting **he** perceives her as a child, but he also blatantly sizes up her up as she shows off her new look at the end of 'The Bomb'. (Steven and Dodo are referred to as a 'couple', a term that almost always denotes a romantic or sexual relationship, three times in *The Celestial Toymaker* and once in *The Ark*.) In *The War Machines* Dodo enthusiastically hits a nightclub with Polly, a liberated young woman who goes out at night and picks up sailors. while it would not be remotely out of the question for a school-age teenager[152] to go clubbing in mid-60s London, no one else in the story, from the Doctor to the thoroughly respectable Sir Charles (who allows Dodo to stay at his home after her night out) or 20-something Polly has an issue with her loud declaration that she wants to go to 'the hottest night spot in town!' If we wish to take Dodo's hugely variable accent into account[153], we might intuit that she was from Northern England but moved to London (perhaps after her mother died, when she came to live with her great-aunt) or that, it being 1965, she just likes doing really bad impressions of the Beatles.

---

[151] This is in part an in-joke: Lane auditioned to play Susan during the casting sessions for **Doctor Who**'s original regulars.

[152] School leaving age in England and Wales was 15 until 1971, although in practice many young people left education before their 15th birthday throughout the 1960s. Jackie Lane celebrated her 25th birthday during her time on **Doctor Who**.

[153] Wiles cast Lane because he had seen her play a Mancunian schoolgirl at the Palace Theatre, Manchester during his own tenure there.

That's certainly possible; Dodo differs from all her predecessors as **Doctor Who**'s female lead in that she's entirely located in the then modern world. In *The Celestial Toymaker* she sports a Dylan cap, a hooped top and a miniskirt: an outfit you can easily imagine on Jo Grant or Clara Oswald, but not Barbara or Vicki. In *The Ark* she uses Beatle slang ('Gear!') and talks about a school trip to Whipsnade (a place surely familiar to much of **Doctor Who**'s audience from exactly that sort of trip, or at least from features on **Blue Peter**). Ian and Barbara are grown-ups, in loco parentis to the audience. Vicki, Steven and Sara are from the future and Katarina is from Troy, while Susan is an unearthly child. Dodo, though, is a thoroughly modern Miss. For the first time in **Doctor Who**, we have a companion who comes from real life.

Right from her first scene, Jackie Lane creates someone distinctive and relatable despite being hampered by conflicting direction about the accent she should play the character with, and makes Dodo, bright, quick, compassionate, and funny. There's also genuine chemistry within the Hartnell-Purves-Lane trio and Dodo, as a swinging 60s Londoner, contrasts far better with Steven Taylor, Pilot of the Future, than Vicki the 25th-century orphan did. (The same applies with the Jamie/Zoe team, which works better than Jamie/Victoria for exactly the same reason. 'The girl is from the future and the boy is from the past?' asks an incredulous German soldier in *The War Games* (1969). Yes, indeed. And that contrast, or its mirror image, is a useful one.)

The archetypal **Doctor Who** companion is a fashionable woman from contemporary Earth (often contemporary London) who is attractive to the audience both as an identification figure and, frankly, an object of lust. She usually has a (sometimes frustrated) desire to do great things, a complicated family background and is strongly empathetic in order to provide a contrast with the more alien aspects of the Doctor.

Whatever the merits or otherwise of that character type, it's fair to say that most casual viewers of modern **Doctor Who** would recognise this as a description of Rose, Martha, Donna, Amy and Clara, but it also applies to Ace, Peri, Tegan, Polly, Jo Grant and Sarah Jane Smith. Dodo is the first **Doctor Who** regular character to demonstrate any aspects of this character type.

Innes Lloyd wrote to Lane after she finished work on **Doctor Who**, specifically tell her that she'd done nothing wrong, and that she was a victim of circumstances. That's disingenuous up to a point, as it was his decision not to continue to employ her, and keeping her in the job was within his gift, but it nevertheless points to something important. Early ideas for *The War Machines* retained Dodo and paired her with a character called Rich, a prototype version of the Ben Jackson character introduced in the transmitted story. Rich and Dodo were to be what Ben and Polly ultimately were, a pair of **Doctor Who** companions from contemporary London who reflected the birth of British cool.

Dodo wasn't being replaced by a completely different sort of character, she was being replaced with a new but actually very similar character, one who is superficially distinct but actually duplicates a lot of Dodo's innovatory contemporary appeal. They are, in fact, so similar, that Dodo very nearly stayed on to do Polly's job for her. It may be that Dodo's origin as another orphan figure and granddaughter substitute prevented her from completely fulfilling the role Polly occupied and which remains the **Doctor Who** companion archetype to this day, but she is not merely a step towards it, she is its first exponent.

Dodo is one of the most important characters in the entire history of **Doctor Who**.

APPENDIX 3: THE FAMILY CHAPLET

In the final scene of 'Bell of Doom' Steven speculates that Dodo's surname being 'Chaplet' and the French grandfather she mentions implies that she is 'Anne's great, great...' and the Doctor concurs. The idea does, after all, validate his point that '...it is possible, of course, that she didn't die, and I was right to leave her', but there is more to it than that.

This could be taken to be a wildly implausible coincidence on two fronts. Firstly that the TARDIS not only takes the Doctor and Steven to one of Anne's descendants, but does so immediately, and second that Anne should have descendants in (then) contemporary London. Tosh has indicated that the end of the serial is meant to indicate that 'We can't be sure if Anne survived but the suggestion was that she did'[154].

With regard to the first point: In the 2011 **Doctor Who** story *The Doctor's Wife*, the TARDIS takes on human form and in response to the Doctor's objection that the TARDIS never took him where he wanted to go, she informs him that while that is true, she often took him 'where you needed to go'. To cite 'Bell of Doom' as an example of this much-later-introduced character point might be thought a stretch, and a massive exercise in both retroactive continuity and narrative hand-waving. Yet it is surely legitimate to regard **Doctor Who** as a single large text, especially given fan involvement in the series' production, and by 2011 the writing and

---

[154] Hearn, 'Script Editing Who, Donald Tosh'.

production of TV **Doctor Who** had been under the executive control of fans with a detailed knowledge of the minutiae of the series' history for the best part of a decade.

The second point is more complex. It is undeniably true that the events of late 1572 led to a mass migration of Huguenots from France to England. They mostly went through Calais, and along roads through Canterbury before largely settling in London, where there is a dispersed but not numerically insignificant community of descendants of French Huguenots. Indeed, still existing organisations such as the Huguenot Church in Soho Square, London and the Huguenot Society of Great Britain and Ireland trace their origins to this period. Dodo, with her French grandfather and French surname could easily be a part of this diaspora.

However, there is also the problem that a descendent of a married Anne would not carry the surname Chaplet, due to surnames being agnatic. Tosh has suggested that Anne married 'The son of her father's cousin'[155], but there is a cleaner solution presented by the serial itself. Anne is sent to her aunt's house. If said aunt is the wife of her father's brother and has a son, she could easily marry a first cousin named Chaplet on the long journey from Paris to Canterbury. (Marriages of this level of consanguinity were hardly rare in early modern France.) Lucarotti, however, used his novelisation to suggest that Dodo was not descended from Anne at all, but from her brother Raoul with whom she escapes from Paris, and who appears in the novelisation but is not even mentioned in the scripts. (This, however, creates the wrinkle that the brother with whom Anne was travelling having 20th-century descendants

---

[155] Hearn, 'Script Editing Who, Donald Tosh'.

does not prove Anne survived the Massacre, it merely implies it. **She** may have died in the violence, which continued for months. However, the novelisation's Anne is in less immediate peril than the TV serial's, due to the Doctor's intervention in procuring her family passes out of the city and advising them to head to Picardy, where the Governor actively used the forces of the state to protect the Huguenot population within his jurisdiction and where violence was consequently minor by comparison. It is not coincidental that Picardy was the birthplace of the then recently dead John Calvin.)

The idea has been raised that as well as looking like Susan, and being a descendant of Anne's, Dodo is also **Steven's** descendant. The theory relies on the idea that Steven and Anne shared more than lodging on the 21 August, when they both stayed in Preslin's shop[156]. Donald Tosh, who wrote the scenes concerned, has dismissed this idea, but it is not impossible, taking the text in isolation, although Steven and Anne's attitude to each other as 'Priest of Death' opens is hard to interpret as the fond conversation of lovers, and there is exactly as much textual suggestion that Steven has spent a night of passion with Nicholas between the first two episodes as there is that he has had one with Anne between the second and third.. (Compare with Ian and Barbara at the beginning of 'The Slave Traders' (*The Romans* episode 1, 1965), for an example of how an obviously post-coital scene could be written and played without disrupting the conventions of 1960s **Doctor Who**.)

There are also several occasions in the script when Steven calls Anne a 'child' which are modified by Purves in delivery to be 'girl'.

---

[156] Wood and Miles, *About Time*, pp231, 233.

This could be seen to support or disaffirm the contention, depending on your point of view. Is Purves changing the lines because he is playing against a woman of his own age[157], and implying a physical relationship between their characters? Annette Robertson was 25 at the time and had recently been married to future **Doctor Who** John Hurt. In 1965 she had starred in two plays as part of the BBC One strand **Monitor** for her lover Ken Russell. Peter Purves turned 27 the day before 'Bell of Doom' was recorded (and two days before 'The Sea Beggar' was transmitted). It may be that in light of the minimal age gap between the two, and Robertson's association with roles vastly more sexually frank than any in **Doctor Who**, that playing Anne as a minor was untenable in performance. Alternatively, some could argue that Tosh's scripting 'child' in the first place rules this interpretation out.

(Lucarotti's novelisation has a more flirtatious relationship between Steven and Anne, e.g. '"I'll be safe with you," she replied beguilingly'[158] and this paragraph:

> 'Steven studied Anne's face for a few moments. Her fresh complexion was surrounded by a shoulder-length tangle of auburn curls, her nose retroussé, and under it a mouth which frequently twitched at the corners as though she were about to burst out laughing, or giggling, at any moment although her pale blue eyes were shrewd and knowing.
>
> '"How old did you say you were?" Steven asked.'[159]

---

[157] Anne is 'fifteen' in Lucarotti's novelisation (p89).
[158] Lucarotti, *Doctor Who: The Massacre*, p76.

It may be that lines earlier in the story that allude to a growing affection between Steven and Anne, e.g. 'You were kind to me. The first one as ever was.' in 'The Sea Beggar', are left over from Lucarotti's draft. They are in a pre-filmed segment, which would have been amongst the first material shot for the story and so could have been spared rewriting if timing was tight.)

Anne being pregnant with Steven's child when she escapes to England would solve the issue of her issue carrying her surname, and given the thousands of French Huguenot refugees who arrived in England without documentation of any kind across the 1570s, her affecting to be a young widow whose husband was one of the tens of thousands who died in the Massacre would hardly be a difficult deception to accomplish.

There is another issue in relation to this, which is of some interest. All humans have two parents, which means that in theory they will have four grandparents, eight great-grandparents, 16 great-great-grandparents, and so on. The number of anyone's ancestors doubles with every generation moving away from them back through history. This means that, if we decide that 'G' is the number of generations we're going back, the number of ancestors any human has in that generation is 2^G, 2 raised to the Gth power.

If a generation is 25 years, then 250 years is ten generations. Two to the power of ten is 1024. This means if you fill in an ancestry chart going back ten generations you need to fill in 1024 names in the tenth generation.

---

[159] Lucarotti, *Doctor Who: The Massacre*, p89.

If Dodo is in her late teens in 'Bell of Doom', and thus born around 1950, then approximately 375 years, or 15 generations, separate her from any child of Anne's. Dodo has about 32,800 ancestors in Anne's generation. Given Dodo's French ancestry it is far more likely than not that they are related, even if Anne is not a direct ancestor of Dodo's. (This may be what Lucarotti was driving at with the introduction of Raoul.)

More strikingly, 1,000 years, on the same scale, is 40 generations. Over 1,000 years everyone has 2 to the power of 40 ancestors, and 2^{40} is about a trillion. This means if you fill in an ancestry chart going back 40 generations you need to fill in around a trillion names in the 40th generation.

This is a problem, because there are not at present, nor have there ever been, a trillion people alive on the planet Earth at any one time. The total global human population circa 2015 is circa 7 billion. At circa 1575 it was around 475 million. (No estimate of the cumulative human population of the world throughout history is much above 100 billion; around a tenth of the number of everyone's ancestors after a mere 1,000 years.)

This means that someone born 1,000 years after 1575 would have everyone who was alive in 1575 in their ancestry chart around 2,000 times; and that's assuming that everyone alive in 1575 had issue and a line of descendants that continued for 1,000 years, which by no means all of them will have. This, of course, means that those people who did have descendants alive 1,000 years in the future would appear many, many more than 2,000 times.

'Bell of Doom' may intend us to conclude that Dodo is a descendent of Anne's, and it is possible that she is also a descendent of

Steven's. However, it is all but mathematically inevitable that if Anne did survive, and has descendants alive in Steven's time, that Steven is a descendent of hers; their births being separated by 1,000 years.

APPENDIX 4: A NOTE ON ETYMOLOGY

Despite its presence in the title of this serial the word 'massacre' is only used twice during it. The first time is by Nicholas in 'The Sea Beggar', when he is describing events at Vassy, and the second by the Doctor at the conclusion of 'Bell of Doom'.

In Middle French (c1100s) 'maçacre' is a word related to the killing of animals for meat, associated with a slaughterhouse, a chopping (or butcher's) block, and the board from which meat was sold by tradesmen[160]. This was possibly derived from, and certainly related to, the Classical Latin 'macellum' (provision shop) and its post-Classical derivation 'macella'. By Early Modern French 'massacre' had, as both a verb and a noun, come to mean the indiscriminate killing of humans and was widely used by Francophones in the 1570s.

However, at the time the serial is set, the word 'massacre' did not exist in English, and was imported into English as a result of the events portrayed at its climax, probably by Huguenot refugees, who came to Protestant England in their thousands. There are no known uses of it as a noun in English before 1578 (when it appears in a pamphlet describing events in Paris in August 1572), with its first appearance as a verb ten years later. For decades afterwards

---

[160] The etymology of the word is thus analogous to that of the English word 'shambles'. Interestingly, a much later Doctor Who story, *Resurrection of the Daleks* (1984) sees a character dismiss a massacre in which he has just participated as 'a shambles', perhaps as a kind of etymological joke.

the noun was largely used to describe August 1572, although the verb quickly took on more general uses[161].

Just as the Ancient Greek derived 'holocaust' (literally 'burnt offering'), present in English and French since the 12th century, became, through a coinage of the 1940s, irretrievably associated with the mass exterminations carried out by the Nazi state, so 'massacre' in English is inherently linked to August 1572.

---

[161] Quite possibly prompted by the extensive use of 'massacre' (verb) in Christopher Marlowe's play of which the Massacre (noun) is the subject; using 'massacre' as a verb very quickly becomes a feature of (surviving) early modern drama following this hugely successful play's initial staging. It is notably more often used to denote actions taken by Catholics against Protestants or by the French (usually coded as Catholic) against the English (coded as Protestant) than in any other context.

APPENDIX 5: TITLE FIGHT

As noted earlier in this volume, the first 25 **Doctor Who** serials do not have overall titles shown onscreen. Each episode has its own title (e.g. 'The Powerful Enemy'[162]) and there is no indication which part of a larger episodic narrative any of them are, or what that larger story is called.

Some serials from this era have overall titles recorded on their camera scripts and some do not. Every serial from this period is assigned an overall title or description on some piece of production office paperwork (e.g. a script, commissioning document, copyright, payment or sales form) but consistent adherence to a single criterion to decide on titles is not possible. This forces anyone attempting to compile a list of titles for Serials A to Z to use a variety of sources and criteria. Inconsistency is inherent to the process of deciding what, if anything, these serials are called.

The scripts for this story were commissioned on Friday 9 July 1965. No title is mentioned on the documentation[163]. Receipt of first drafts of all four episodes was acknowledged on Tuesday 20 July, under the title 'The War of God'. This title (with definite article, unlike the final title of the first instalment) was still attached when second drafts were delivered from Tuesday 28 September to Friday 8 October.

---

[162] Now generally considered the first episode of a two-part serial called *The Rescue*.
[163] This is not unusual for the period.

A production schedule almost certainly drafted in early October (it allocates VT numbers[164] to episodes up to 'Devil's Planet' (*The Daleks' Master Plan* episode 3, 1965)) gives the title as 'The Massacre of St Bartholomew' and has writer, director and (the wrong) designer assigned[165]. There are also undated, unnamed handwritten notes in the production file, presumed to date from this period, which refer to it as 'Dr Who & the Massacre of St Bartholomew (Made up)'[166].

The filming schedules issued to some members of the cast on 22 December 1965 and the accompanying covering letters call the serial 'The Massacre of St Bartholomew'.

Production scripts for the serial's studio recordings in January 1966 call it 'The Massacre of St Bartholomew's Eve', but publicity photographs taken during the studio recording for 'War of God' use 'The Massacre of Saint Bartholomew' (unusually, without abbreviating 'saint').

---

[164] VT numbers: Literally a Video Tape number; an identifier for the magnetic video tape onto which a television programme had been recorded in the studio and (usually) from which it would be transmitted to the nation. A VT number would be allocated soon after recording and by definition could not be allocated before, making it likely this list was created the week between 5 and 12 November 1965.

[165] Pixley, Andrew, 'By Any Other Name'.

[166] Some other serials on this list have '(Made up)' after their titles or descriptions. The meaning is obscure.

The *Radio Times* article for the launch of the serial[167] does not provide a title for the serial, and the weekly listings only give individual episode's titles. This is also true of the PasB forms.

This brings us to the end of the serial's active production.

BBC Enterprises documentation from 1974, offering the serial for sale to overseas markets, gives the title as 'Doctor Who And The Massacre', abbreviating the description of the serial's setting to two words for the first time. (A 'Dr./Dr/Doctor Who &/and' prefix is often applied to **Doctor Who** serials, even ones with onscreen titles, in these sorts of documents.)

A further abbreviated version of **this** abbreviated title, i.e. 'The Massacre', became the preferred form of the serial's title from the 1970s onwards, probably due to its use in the 1976 edition of *The Making of Doctor Who*[168]. (It became standard for *Doctor Who Magazine* and was, for example, carried over to the paperback edition of the 1981 *The Doctor Who Programme Guide*[169], its revised 1989 and 1994 reissues, and the *Radio Times* Twentieth Anniversary Special.)

John Lucarotti's 1987 novelisation of the serial opts for this shorter title also, and both the author in his preface and the copyright information attribute it to the original serial as well as the novella.

From the early 1990s, following research into **Doctor Who**'s earliest days which uncovered the documents from 1965-66 quoted above,

---

[167] *Radio Times*, 5 to 13 February 1966.
[168] Dicks, Terrance and Malcolm Hulke, *The Making of Doctor Who*.
[169] The hardback published earlier the same year eschewed assigning overall titles for stories before *The Savages* (1966).

publications such as *Doctor Who Magazine* opted for the longer 'The Massacre of St Bartholomew's Eve', although other licensed publications (e.g. The Discontinuity Guide) continued to refer to the serial as 'The Massacre'.

It is indicative of the indeterminacy about the serial's title prevalent at the time that the 1998 BBC Radio Collection CD release of the serial's extant audio soundtrack uses 'The Massacre' on the spine and frontispiece, but 'The Massacre of St Bartholomew's Eve' on the disc art and within Peter Purves' narration. (Later reissues amend the disc art to match the cover but, understandably, do not amend the narration.)

Finally, a 2015 CD edition of the novelisation, read by Peter Purves, retains the shorter title of 'The Massacre' for the book but ascribes 'The Massacre of St Bartholomew's Eve' to the TV serial itself.

Much has been made of the 'historical inaccuracy' of the Eve version of the title[170]. It is pointed out that the Massacre in Paris took place on 24 August, St Bartholomew's Day, making the term 'the Massacre of St Bartholomew's Eve' nonsensical. (A cursory google of the phrase demonstrates that the vast majority of hits relate to this **Doctor Who** serial, not the historical events within which it is set, lending support to this view.)

Yet this issue is one solely faced by Anglophones with regard to an event that took place in France, and for which most of the historiographical material is Francophone. (Although it is a problem which is amplified by the very specific context of discussion of **Doctor Who**.)

---

[170] Wood and Miles, *About Time*, p230.

In French the event is referred to consistently as 'le Massacre de la Saint-Barthélemy'. This translates literally as 'the Massacre of Saint Bartholomew'[171]. Saint Bartholomew is a noun, and does not qualify 'Day' or 'Eve'. The phrase is sufficient unto itself in French but not in English. This is the root cause of the problem.

As the Doctor notes in the serial itself, the killing 'continued for several days in Paris and then spread itself to other parts of France'. These later killings, some occurring as later as October, are considered part of 'le Massacre de la Saint-Barthélemy' by Francophone historiography. Also considered part of Saint-Barthélemy are the two attempts, the latter successful, on the life of Gaspard II de Coligny on 22 and 23 August and murders of prominent Huguenots, also on the 23rd, that occurred before the street violence began[172].

Within even a loose and broad understanding of the historical events, discussion of the 'historical accuracy' of the words Eve and Day is unneeded. Huguenots died on both days and for more than 40 days afterwards.

Equally, the term 'The Massacre of St Bartholomew's Eve' is not wholly unknown in English-language responses to the event, although it is more often found when the concentration is on the deaths of aristocrats at the court, some within the Palace itself, on

---

[171] This is, of course, also the title on the October schedule.
[172] The first attempted assassination, which is depicted in 'Priest of Death', could be said to take place on Saint Bartholomew's Eve's Eve, if one (inexplicably) wished to extend the series further in 'antepenultimate' fashion.

the 23rd, rather than the thousands of peasants who died in the streets beginning on the 24th.

The phrase 'The Massacre of Saint Bartholomew's Eve' may have gained currency in English with the publication of *Margaret of Navarre: Or the Massacre of Saint Bartholomew's Eve*[173] in 1846. This was an anonymous pirate two-volume edition of the Dumas novel more usually known as *La Reine Margot*, issued to cash in on the success of the first official English editions of Dumas' D'Artagnan romances. This pirate edition sold in massive quantities throughout the year, but has since been obscured by the standard English version of this text, the later (but also 1846) authorised translation entitled *Marguerite de Valois: An Historical Romance*[174] which is used as the basis for, for example, the Oxford University Press edition into the present century.

Saint Bartholomew's Eve is also the title of a children's fiction by the reactionary Victorian writer George Alfred Henty, published in 1894, and a fragmentary drama written in the 1890s by (the Catholic writer) GK Chesterton[175].

There are various other examples in the latter half of the 19th century and early in the 20th, and they are not confined to fiction. Grace Lawless Lee's seminal *The Huguenot Settlements in Ireland* (1936) mentions 'The Massacre of Saint Bartholomew's Eve' several

---

[173] Dumas, Alexandre, trans unknown, *Margaret of Navarre: Or the Massacre of Saint Bartholomew's Eve*.
[174] Dumas, Alexandre, trans Alexandrine-Sophie Goury de Champgrand, *Marguerite de Valois: An Historical Romance*.
[175] The title is assigned by Chesterton scholarship but the phrase occurs in the work itself.

times[176], indicating it was casual currency in even specialised historical writing that did not directly cover the events. The term also occasionally turns up in the later twentieth century. It is put into Lord Burleigh's mouth in the fourth episode of BBC One's *Elizabeth R*, and appears in more recent popular work, such as Alistair Horne's celebrated *Seven Ages of Paris: Portrait of a City*[177].

However, frequent claims in **Doctor Who**-based writing that the 'Eve' version of Serial W's title indicates that the story is about the build-up to the massacre, rather than the massacre itself, ring hollow with special pleading: an attempt to assert that this **Doctor Who** serial was not named in error. Any Anglophone would naturally interpret something entitled 'The Massacre of Christmas Eve' to be about a massacre that took place on 24 December, not the build-up to a massacre that occurred on Christmas Day. (Equally, 'The Massacre of Christmas' would be assumed by most to refer to 25 December, but might legitimately be taken to refer to the whole Christmas period.)

Donald Tosh continues to refer to the event as 'The Massacre of Saint Bartholomew's Eve'[178], doing so when interviewed about **Doctor Who**'s 50th anniversary and again in 2014, including when interviewed by mainstream media publications rather than those that specialise in discussion of **Doctor Who** (and which therefore

---

[176] Lawless Lee is not easily dismissed. She was a pioneering historian of the documentation of the movement of religious refugees. There are academic prizes, grants and scholarships named in her honour open to students of appropriate disciplines at Trinity College Dublin.

[177] Horne, Alistair, *Seven Ages of Paris: Portrait of a City*.

[178] E.g. in Smith, 'Doctor Who story editor Donald Tosh'.

may have silently 'corrected' his usage). It is a reasonable assumption, then, that this curiosity of translation and tradition was introduced into **Doctor Who** by him.

Thus, while it has clear evidentiary basis in **Doctor Who**'s production history and is not wholly without precedent in terms of the Anglophone responses to the historical event, 'The Massacre of St Bartholomew's Eve' is an ugly, and slightly confused, coinage, possibly arrived at by error, and which is justified by fan scholarship through insisting on an interpretation of it as a phrase that is contrary to standard English usage.

As such, it is of little utility.

Strictly, Serial W is *The Massacre of Saint Bartholomew's Eve*, if the question is 'What is the serial's overall title?' and the criterion for answering it is 'What it says on the top left corner of the camera scripts'. By that criterion, though, the story released on VHS and DVD as *An Unearthly Child* (1963), often referred to on production paperwork as '100,000 BC' and considered by its author to be called 'The Tribe of Gum' is simply 'Serial A' – something no-one would ever attempt to impose on the front of a commercial product.

This volume adopts *The Massacre* as the title of this serial in line with **Black Archive** house style and in the interests of repeating a two-, rather than six-, word title dozens of times throughout the text. This is despite the earliest extant documentation containing this version of the title post-dating the serial's production by a decade, and being unconnected with the **Doctor Who** production office.

So there.

APPENDIX 6: RECEPTION AND RATINGS[179]

Detailed contemporary responses to individual **Doctor Who** stories of the 1960s are relatively rare. As a programme intended, at least in part, for children, and broadcast before prime time, it was unusual for episodes or serials to singled out and reviewed individually[180]. Even when they were, the actual copy would actually be fairly generic, with a sentence or two about the episode ostensibly reviewed, and then more general comments about the series as a whole. This stands in stark contrast to the often exhausting, and exponentially speedily appearing, analysis applied to **Doctor Who** on transmission since the early 1980s.

The Massacre is a story that was subject to something approaching an individual review, albeit one that contains little more than a sentence about the actual story, in the *Daily Worker* of Saturday 5 February 1966. Stewart Lane wrote of:

> 'the programme moving to 16th-century Paris, with plotting between the Catholics and Huguenot, but I fear the Daleks may return yet again. After all, the BBC has already granted 60 licences for the production of Dalek

---

[179] For further viewing figures, please visit
http://www.obversebooks.co.uk/blackarchive/viewing.html.
[180] This is in part a function of the inherent unavailability of preview copies of episodes before screenings; an episode could only be reviewed after it was shown, and a piece tying into broadcast could not actually engage with the episode being broadcast.

toys, with still more being negotiated, and it gets 5 per cent of the wholesale price of each toy!'[181]

Of more interest though is his comment that that:

'**Doctor Who**, now in its "third successful year", is definitely showing signs of age and my spies have it that even the youngsters are getting tired of it.'

To someone reading (or writing) about **Doctor Who** after its golden jubilee celebrations, the idea that it might have run out of steam a little more than two years into its run seems absurd. However, this contemporary comment should not be dismissed wholly out of hand, as Lane's perception of **Doctor Who**'s declining powers and appeal coincided, in a way he cannot have been aware of when he wrote, with a collapse in the number of people watching **Doctor Who**, with more than 25% of the serial's initial audience disappearing before its end:

'War of God'   8.0 million

'The Sea Beggar'   6.0 million

'Priest of Death'   5.9 million

'Bell of Doom'   5.8 million[182]

---

[181] The *Daily Worker*, founded in 1930 by the Communist Party of Great Britain, is now the *Morning Star*. In the 1960s it was a mass market tabloid with a sizeable readership. It would often allow its political underpinnings to influence its entertainment coverage, as here. (Something in which it differs from exactly no other newspapers.)

The Massacre is both the first **Doctor Who** serial of more than two episodes' duration to lose viewers between every episode, and one of only a handful of serials of which this is true[183]. Television viewing figures are, of course, not an indicator of quality, but they are a legitimate indicator of popularity and audience engagement, especially when qualified by appropriate context.

In the weeks immediately before the serial, ten of the 12 episodes of *The Daleks' Master Plan* drew over 9 million viewers, and one

---

[182] See, among other sources, Howe, David, Stammers, Mark, and Walker, Stephen James, *Doctor Who: The Handbook – The First Doctor*, p118.

[183] The others are *The Underwater Menace*, *Robot* (1974-5), *Warriors of the Deep* (1984), *The Twin Dilemma* (1984) and *Dragonfire* (1987) (Howe, Stammers and Walker, *Doctor Who: The Handbook – The Second Doctor*, p52; Howe, David, Stammers, Mark, and Walker, Stephen James, *Doctor Who: The Handbook – The Fourth Doctor*, p54; Howe, David, Stammers, Mark, and Walker, Stephen James, *Doctor Who: The Handbook – The Fifth Doctor*, p128; Howe, David, Stammers, Mark, and Walker, Stephen James, *Doctor Who: The Handbook – The Sixth Doctor*, p73; Howe, David, Stammers, Mark, and Walker, Stephen James, *Doctor Who: The Handbook – The Seventh Doctor*, p52;). *Robot* is an outlier in the list, and needs to be seen in context: it started from a very high base (10.8m) at the end of a calendar year, 1974, that had seen **Doctor Who**'s best ratings since 1965. It was immediately followed by *The Ark in Space* (1975), the second episode of which finally beat *The Web Planet*'s record from almost exactly 10 years before (Howe, Stammers and Walker, *The Handbook – The Fourth Doctor*, p45). Curiously, although the scripts were written by Robert Holmes, *The Ark in Space* was based upon a story idea by John Lucarotti, his first contribution to Doctor Who since the spat over *The Massacre*.

over 10 million[184]. The fall is even more striking when we compare the figures for these episodes with those for the equivalent weeks a year and two years earlier.

	1964		1965		1966	
Week 6	'The Edge of Destruction'[185]	10.4	'Inferno'[186]	12	'War of God'	8.0
Week 7	'The Brink of Disaster'[187]	9.9	'The Web Planet'[188]	13.5	'The Sea Beggar'	6.0
Week 8	'The Roof of the World'[189]	9.4	'The Zarbi'[190]	12.5	'Priest of Death'	5.9
Week 9	'The Singing Sands'[191]	9.4	'Escape to Danger'[192]	12.5	'Bell of Doom'	5.8

NB: Viewing figures in millions.[193]

---

[184] Howe, Stammers and Walker, *The Handbook – The First Doctor*, p114.
[185] *The Edge of Destruction* episode 1.
[186] *The Romans* episode 4.
[187] *The Edge of Destruction* episode 2.
[188] *The Web Planet* episode 1.
[189] *Marco Polo* episode 1.
[190] *The Web Planet* episode 2.
[191] *Marco Polo* episode 2.
[192] *The Web Planet* episode 3.
[193] Howe, Stammers and Walker, *The Handbook – The First Doctor*, pp63, 65, 88, 91, 118.

February into March had previously been **Doctor Who**'s peak ratings period for the calendar year. The episodes shown these weeks in 1964 and 1965 are directly comparable with those that comprise *The Massacre* in other ways too. In 1964 and 1966 they are the episodes immediately following a Dalek story, while in 1965 five episodes separate Week 6 from a Dalek instalment. All three years see examples of the ostensibly less popular historical episodes of **Doctor Who** transmitted in some of these weeks, although 1966 is the only year in which they occupy all four of these weeks[194].

However, *The Romans* (1965), coming off the back of a Dalek serial with a two-week interlude, has an average of 11.6 million viewers per episode, which compares favourably with the Dalek story's 11.9 million[195]. A year before, *Marco Polo*, following on from *The Daleks* (1963-64), also with a two week interlude, averages at 9.4 million viewers, which is actually higher than *The Daleks'* own average of 8.9 million[196].

---

[194] Shuffling episodes of *The Romans* or *Marco Polo* 'up' to compare historical episodes directly with *The Massacre* does the later story no favours. Indeed *The Romans* (13 million, 11.5 million, 10 million, 12 million (Howe, Stammers and Walker, *The Handbook – The First Doctor*, p88)) remains one of the most watched **Doctor Who** serials ever transmitted into the 21st century.

[195] Howe, Stammers and Walker, *The Handbook – The First Doctor*, p88. The two-part serial between them (*The Rescue* (1965), comprising 'The Powerful Enemy' and 'Desperate Measures') has an average of 12.5 million (Howe, Stammers and Walker, *The Handbook – The First Doctor*, p85), beating them both.

[196] Howe, Stammers and Walker, *The Handbook – The First Doctor*, pp58, 65. The two part serial between them (*The Edge of*

Whether the audiences would have been drawn to **Doctor Who** in the first place without the Daleks' presence is beside the point; in 1964 and 1965 the episodes, historical or otherwise, that followed that January's Dalek serial were capable of retaining the audience who tuned in to see Daleks a few weeks before. It is by no means standard for **Doctor Who**'s 1960s audience to abandon the series en masse as the Daleks glide off the screen.

The substantial fall is between the first two episodes of *The Massacre*, with smaller increments of audience abandonment between the remaining instalments. Yet these steps down cumulatively result in 'Bell of Doom' drawing the series' smallest audience since the week of its first transmission[197]. (The next episode, 'The Steel Sky' fell further to 5.5 million viewers[198], at which point the series' downward trajectory stopped and the series made a modest recovery that would last until the summer.)

Since the emergence of a good-quality recording of the soundtrack of the serial in the 1990s, the reputation of this serial, at least

---

Destruction (1964), comprising 'The Edge of Destruction' and 'The Brink of Disaster') has an average of 10.1 million (Howe, Stammers and Walker, *The Handbook – The First Doctor*, p63), beating them both.

[197] 'An Unearthly Child' (*An Unearthly Child* episode 1 (1963)), famously shown the day after the assassination of President Kennedy, drew a very small audience (4.4 million). The exceptional circumstances were acknowledged by the BBC, who repeated the episode a week later, immediately before 'The Cave of Skulls' (*An Unearthly Child* episode 2 (1963), when both episodes rated much better (5.9 million).

[198] Howe, Stammers and Walker, *The Handbook – The First Doctor*, p120.

amongst **Doctor Who** fans and within media devoted to the discussion of **Doctor Who**, has grown. *The Discontinuity Guide* suggested that it might be 'the best' **Doctor Who** serial, due to its serious engagement with a difficult subject, while *About Time*[199] and *Running Through Corridors*[200] also praised its sense of purpose and the quality of its acting and writing.

If we are to assume that the collapse of **Doctor Who**'s audience during *The Massacre* was not coincidental[201], it is worth asking what on Earth about it managed to drive 2.2 million viewers away between 'War of God' and 'Bell of Doom', and what about 'Bell of Doom' persuaded a further 0.5 million to not bother tuning in for the next story, in case it was too much like it.

While we cannot be certain, with no copy to view, that the production is visually effective, the serial makes no demands of the television production technology of 1965 that **Doctor Who** was not easily capable of satisfying[202]. (Peter Purves has commented that: 'The costumes alone were amazing. The atmosphere, I remember, was absolute fantastic, but I've no evidence of what it looked like.'[203])

---

[199] Wood and Miles, *About Time*, p 233-236.

[200] Shearman, Robert, and Toby Hadoke, *Running Through Corridors: Rob and Toby's Marathon Watch of Doctor Who – Volume 1: The 60s*, pp136-37.

[201] If we're not to assume that, then this appendix ends here.

[202] A friend, who shall remain nameless, speculated that much of the cast spent the serial naked, acting against black drapes, and that the audience was repulsed by this combination of pornography and anti-mimesis. It's a sadly implausible theory.

[203] Adams, Matt, 'Taking the Lead', DWM #483.

The extant audio track is of an atmospheric, well-acted piece, with a lot of very good dialogue and an essential moral seriousness in how it engages with what are undoubtedly serious matters that is both striking and compulsive.

It may be that the very qualities that make this serial admirable and interesting in retrospect are precisely the reasons it drove away **Doctor Who**'s audience. Those who listen to the soundtrack of a 'missing' piece of television, or read the scripts for the same, have already made a prior commitment to the material, and a fairly deep one at that. They are not simply prepared to look beyond the obvious, they **have** to in order to experience something that at present only exists outside its own medium.

The Massacre is unusual in many respects. The series' lead character disappears for the middle two weeks and for those weeks replaced by a sinister singsong doppelganger who only appears in three scenes across those two episodes, in one of which he does not speak. He is then brutally murdered at the end of the third. Peter Purves rises admirably to the occasion, and more than fulfils the demands made upon him as a performer following Steven's elevation to sole lead, but his character is alienated, alone and confused for almost the entire story. (Indeed this is part of why Purves' performance is so powerful.) 'The Sea Beggar' in particular is a circumlocutionary script, one in which its lead character is constantly frustrated, denied agency and understanding, and in which almost nothing happens. The piece cuts away from these events to a parallel storyline that never quite intersects with Steven's story. It involves long scenes exclusively populated by the French aristocracy, entirely represented by characters who never meet Steven or the Doctor, some of whom only appear in one episode. They repeatedly rehash a single argument about religious and political issues, none of which are ever **quite** fully articulated to the audience.

John Wiles, although not speaking of *The Massacre* specifically but of his time on **Doctor Who** more generally, once commented, 'The more depth you give to a thing… the more seriousness with which you view it… the more impossible it becomes on the screen, and the more unviewable'[204]. These are - as far as we can tell in the absence of copies anyway - alienating pieces of television; should we be surprised that they alienated a quarter of the audience? Gerry Davis, the credited Story Editor on 'Bell of Doom', later went on to co-create the Cybermen, **Doctor Who**'s second most popular monster race. For this he found himself feted by **Doctor Who** fandom in the 1980s and was frequently and extensively interviewed for his thoughts on the series' history and (then) present. He often imparted the information that he and Lloyd had joined **Doctor Who** at a point when its ratings were in dire straits, and that they were instructed to turn the situation around or face the series being cancelled.

This may be what Davis remembered about his arrival in the production office 20 years earlier, but it cannot be the case. While Lloyd and Davis may have felt pressured by the series' sudden ratings drop, they were appointed before it occurred, which makes it impossible that their appointment was a response to it.

Whether it truly was their brief or not, Lloyd and Davis failed to revive **Doctor Who**'s ratings, which would not recover in the

---

[204] McLachlan, Ian, 'The John Wiles Interview Part 2'.

monochrome era[205]. If episodes shown after *The Massacre* are compared not with the episodes immediately before and after them, but instead with episodes transmitted in the same week (and almost always the same slot) in the years before *The Massacre*, then there can be no other conclusion.

There are 147 episodes of 60s **Doctor Who after** *The Massacre*; on only 20 occasions did any of these episodes out-rate their week/slot counterparts from **before** *The Massacre*. Even this number flatters the series. The majority of those occasions (13) are of episodes out-rating their counterparts from November and December 1963, before the Daleks came along and made **Doctor Who** a ratings success. Three of them are an episode out-rating **Doctor Who**'s scarcely-watched first instalment.

Let's use another measure. There were around one hundred episodes of **Doctor Who** before *The Massacre*. Well over half of them were seen by 9 million people or more. After it, the series would only crack the 9 million barrier twice in 147 attempts. The next **Doctor Who** episode to get more than 10 million viewers would be a Christmas compilation repeat of *The Dæmons* (1971) shown on 28 December 1971 nearly six years later[206], when the audience had arguably undergone a generational renewal.

---

[205] To the extent that the most watched episodes of **Doctor Who** with Patrick Troughton in are from *The Three Doctors*, and the most watched story on which he has a credit is *The Day of the Doctor*.

[206] Howe, David, Stammers, Mark, and Walker, Stephen James, *Doctor Who: The Handbook – The Third Doctor*, p 89

Perhaps Lane's belief that 'even the youngsters are getting tired of it' was not as wide of the mark as our distant posterity makes it seem.

APPENDIX 7: THE END OF HISTORY

Producer Innes Lloyd and Story Editor Gerry Davis, waiting in the wings as *The Massacre* was produced, quickly dispensed with the 'past' serials of which it was an example. Lloyd told the magazine *Television Today*: 'One change we have decided to make is to drop the historical stories because we found they weren't very popular.'[207]

While it is a matter of interpretation whether an assessment of the audience size for the 'past' **Doctor Who** serials as a whole supports this contention, it is more likely that Lloyd was referring to audience appreciation index. This, a separate figure which judges the percentage of a programme's audience who enjoyed it, had for *The Gunfighters*, the then most recent 'past' serial, plumbed new depths, with only 30% of respondents having a positive view of the final episode. It is also worth considering that, with *The Gunfighters* finding new lows in terms of audience engagement eight weeks after *The Massacre* saw the series' overall viewership crashing down, Lloyd was in the position where the two separate metrics he had for measuring audience popularity seemed to indicate more or less simultaneously that Adventures in History, regardless of the tone, style or topic, were the problem.

The Gunfighters was a comical 'past' serial commissioned by Wiles and Tosh and which Lloyd and Davis both later indicated was only made at all because there were no other producible scripts

---

[207] Quoted in Howe, Stammers and Walker, *Doctor Who: The Handbook – The Second Doctor*, p123.

available to them at the time it needed to be shot; only the ruthless treadmill of **Doctor Who**'s weekly production saved that serial from being abandoned.

It has long been observed that the mere two Lloyd/Davis-initiated 'past' serials are patterned after specific works of fiction. *The Smugglers* (1966) mixes elements of Russell Thorndyke's **Doctor Syn** stories (beginning 1915) and J Meade Faulkner's novel *Moonfleet* (1898), and *The Highlanders* is derived from Robert Louis Stevenson's *Kidnapped* (1866). This has been contrasted unfavourably with the variety demonstrated before they took over.

However, there is a visible, and arguably more restrictive, 'house style' for 'past' serials developed during the Wiles/Tosh era of **Doctor Who** which has received less attention. Wiles and Tosh were not in charge of **Doctor Who** for very long. They only commissioned three 'past' serials, from two writers, and the last of these was the aforementioned *The Gunfighters*. However, just as it is immediately noticeable that every science fiction story either commissioned or produced by Wiles/Tosh uses invisibility as a plot point, there is a notable recurring pattern in their three historical adventures.

In all three a historical event which involves a substantial death toll forms the centrepiece of the fourth episode, and the other three build towards that event over a few days. In all three the Doctor is mistaken for someone: Zeus, the Abbot and Doc Holliday respectively. *The Myth Makers* and *The Gunfighters* are both comic stories, and both written by Donald Cotton, which might explain these points of resemblance, but it does not explain their occurrence in *The Massacre*.

What **would** explain their occurrence in *The Massacre*? If the setting of the story was, as Lucarotti remembered, given to him by Tosh rather than being something he himself came up with, and if that setting had been selected, in part, because of how it lent itself to this new house style and structure for 'past' serials.

It should not go unnoted at this point that this common description of *The Myth Makers*, *The Massacre* and *The Gunfighters* also applies to an even earlier **Doctor Who** serial: *The Romans*, written and produced between Lucarotti's second **Doctor Who** serial *The Aztecs* and Tosh's arrival in the production office. In *The Romans*, the Doctor is mistaken for the musician Maximillian Pettulian in the build-up to the Great Fire of Rome of AD 64. This story, written by **Doctor Who**'s second Story Editor, Dennis Spooner, was a considerable success; averaging 11.6 million viewers across its four episodes (indeed it remains one of the 20 most watched **Doctor Who** serials ever made to this day) and it is clearly the basic model for all the Wiles/Tosh era 'past' serials.

There are further similarities between *The Massacre* and *The Gunfighters*, often considered poles apart as **Doctor Who** serials, that speak further of a unified approach to historical drama or suggest a common point of origin. For example: in both, the first and second episodes are bridged by scenes in which the Doctor tells his companion(s) to wait in a local drinking den while he meets a local historical celebrity with medical knowledge; and both generate incident by having the Doctor, as in *The Romans*, initially ignorant of the bloody event that concludes the serial.

The Massacre and *The Gunfighters* are the two **Doctor Who** stories that contain the largest number of genuine historical figures as speaking characters. This is striking in itself, but both also leave out real people who were at the historical events portrayed, and contributed significantly to them, while also showing completely fictional people (e.g. Charles Preslin, Seth Harper) as being central to them. On top of that, both stories also take real historical people with no known connection to those events and place them within them as key figures.

Interestingly, almost all *The Gunfighters'* diversions from the historical record can be traced to the 1957 film *Gunfight at the OK Corral*, directed by John Sturges. Some of these are plausibly the result of different writers making the same decisions (e.g. both the film and **Doctor Who** kill Ike and Phineas Clanton at the OK Corral when neither died there – Ike was present, but survived and died in 1900, whereas Phineas wasn't in Tombstone at the time, and died of pneumonia in 1906), but some are, quite frankly, not. For example, the changing of the historical Kate Elder's surname to Fisher and a scene in which Doc Holliday berates the dying Johnny Ringo. (This point of similarity is particularly striking, in that Sturges' film was the first iteration of the Tombstone story to include Ringo, a historical figure who was not, in reality, present at these events and had no real connection with them.)

Furthermore, the interior set for the Last Chance Saloon of *The Gunfighters* is clearly modelled on the saloon from *Gunfight at the OK Corral* and even principally shot from the same angle. This is also true of the exterior set for the Saloon's entrance, with the end of 'A Holiday for the Doctor' (episode 1) being one of several scenes in *The Gunfighters* that spoofs a specific shot from Sturges' film. *Gunfight at the OK Corral* is also notable for being a film which uses a song about the events it portrays to in part drive, in part narrate and in part comment on its plot. This is a device also utilised in *The Gunfighters*.

How is *The Gunfighters'* clear derivation from John Sturges' film relevant to *The Massacre*? Well, as all three Wiles/Tosh historical stories are clearly derived from *The Romans*, and *The Gunfighters* is additionally patterned after a popular film, the fact that *The Romans* too is overtly patterned after a then-recent Hollywood motion picture (1954's *Quo Vadis*) takes on increased relevance.

Let's return to those final two 'past' serials made by Lloyd and Davis. *The Smugglers* borrows as much from the 1955 *Moonfleet* film as it does either Thorndyke's or Faulkner's texts, and *The Highlanders* was also suggested by John Prebble's factual book *Culloden* (1962) which was adapted into a television play by Peter Watkins and shown on the BBC in 1964. We thus have a situation where most **Doctor Who** historical stories made after early 1965 are derived from either *The Romans* or a notable recent historical drama or both, and *The Massacre* is not an exception.

There is a 1954 film of Dumas' novel *La Reine Margot*, also known in English as *A Woman of Evil*. Devoting more of its narrative to the events of August 1572 than the novel from which it is derived, the film begins in a tavern, where an argument about religious differences and an insult to the Princess Margaret threatens to become violent, a scene that does not appear in the source novel. The film's depiction of the shooting of Admiral de Coligny has him, as in *The Massacre*, stoop to pick up papers at the moment when Bondot fires. The serial's portrayal of Catherine de Medici as the overtly Machiavellian instigator of the Massacre owes something to the film's (she is the woman of the alternative title) and Jean

Young's performance seems to nod towards Francois Rosay's seething portrayal, while the resemblances between the performances of Robert Porte and Barry Justice are not wholly dismissible by countering that they are both playing the same historical figure. Significantly, both tellings also take care to portray the common people of Paris as on the brink of exploding into violence.

There are also substantial differences between *The Massacre* and *A Woman of Evil*, of course. The principal characters of the latter are Princess Margaret and Henry of Navarre, neither of whom appear in the **Doctor Who** serial, and like the source novel, Jean Dreville's film continues its narrative for more than two years after 24 August 1572.

It is interesting to ponder whether, given the visual nods to *Gunfight at the OK Corral* that litter *The Gunfighters*, the same is true of *La Reine Margot* and *The Massacre*, in terms of costume choices and set elements, if not the actual shots called by the director.

The final 'past' **Doctor Who** story, *The Highlanders*, was transmitted less than eleven months after 'Bell of Doom'[208] with only *The Gunfighters* and *The Smugglers* in the interim. Indeed, it seems likely[209] that *The Highlanders* itself only happened because

---

[208] An argument is often made for *Black Orchid* (1982) being a brief revival of the form but if it is so, it's on a technicality. The serial is a literary pastiche in which the TARDIS itself plays a crucial role, and was not made to satisfy the remit of 'past' stories as laid down by **Doctor Who**'s original production team.
[209] Pixley, Andrew, 'Archive: The Highlanders', DWM #292.

retiring BBC executive Elwyn Jones expressed an interest in writing a **Doctor Who** serial, but only of the type being phased out. In the end Jones did no work on the story, and Story Editor Gerry Davis had to put scripts for the serial together himself with very little notice.

The blame for **Doctor Who**'s ratings crash would not be attached by fan history to *The Massacre*, or a combination of it and *The Gunfighters*, but instead to *The Gunfighters* alone, which would find itself routinely described as one of the least effective of all **Doctor Who** serials[210]. (Fortunately that serial survives in its entirety and has been considerably reassessed[211] since it became available to those interested in **Doctor Who**, via showings on repeat channel UK Gold and commercial VHS, DVD and even CD releases.) Intriguingly, Wiles indicated when interviewed in 1981 that with regards to *The Massacre* 'I have an idea it put the lid on all history-pieces. A directive came through that the Doctor would not travel back in time ever again.'[212] If such a directive was issued, it was either not on paper originally or a copy of such does not survive. It would, however, put Lloyd's decision to abandon such serials in a different light. In his *Television Today* interview Lloyd commented that the abandonment of the 'past' stories wouldn't

---

[210] E.g. Haining, Peter, *Doctor Who: A Celebration*, p180, 'Sid The Rat', '25 Five Years Of Turkeys', DWM #144; Paul J Smith, 'The Season Survey Results', DWM #150.
[211] E.g. Cornell, Day and Topping, *The Discontinuity Guide*, p57; Shearman and Hadoke, *Running through Corridors*, pp151-56.
[212] McLachlan, Ian, 'The John Wiles Interview Part 2'.

'mean we won't use historical backgrounds'[213] although in the event, after *The Highlanders* **Doctor Who** would move further and further away from its original format of alternating 'past' and 'future' stories, rarely even using the Earth's history as the setting for monster-based serials. Only two further monochrome adventures (*The Evil of the Daleks* (1967) and *The Abominable Snowmen* (1967)) are set, even partially, in Earth's history[214] and over six years passed between *The Abominable Snowmen* and the first colour story with a (nominally) historical setting, *The Time Warrior* (1973-74)[215]. This would be less surprising if the directive Wiles referred to had indeed been issued.

It is perhaps relevant that in that *Television Today* interview Lloyd does not specify with whom 'past' serials were unpopular. He may be slyly referring to the simple fact that they were unpopular with the new inhabitants of the production office themselves – and perhaps, in light of Wiles' comments about a directive, their superiors as well?

---

[213] Quoted in Howe, Stammers, and Walker, *Doctor Who: The Handbook – The Second Doctor*, p123.

[214] Although *The War Games* initially affects to be set in human history, before revealing that the time travellers are on an alien world as does *Carnival of Monsters* (1973). Both indicate that even when Doctor Who wanted to use the furniture of a historical setting, it felt compelled to detach it from the period. Additionally we discover in the last episode of *The Faceless Ones* (1967) that the serial is set a year before its transmission.

[215] The Atlantis of *The Time Monster* (1972) cannot be called a historical setting by any reasonable measure, even if it is nominally the past.

Thereafter **Doctor Who** would utilise historical settings on average once a year for the rest of its 20th-century run, although several further years (e.g. 1978, 1980, 1986) would pass with no stories set in the past, and producer John Nathan-Turner would later indicate that he now considered serials set in the middle decades of the 20th century, and even around the time that **Doctor Who** began production, to constitute 'historicals'[216]. It would only be in the 21st century that the revived **Doctor Who** would conspicuously engage with the time travel aspect of its format once again, and even then without producing episodes where the historical setting was not under threat from something from another planet, place or time.

---

[216] Stephens, Adam, and Matthew Brooke, 'The Show Must Go On', DWM #487.

BIBLIOGRAPHY

Books

Aubert de La Chesnaye-Desbois, Francois Alexander Badier, *Dictionnaire de la Noblesse*. Paris, Schelesinger Frères, 1869.

Baird, Henry M, *History of the Rise of the Huguenots* vol 2. London, Hodder & Stoughton, 1879.

Bourgeon, Jean-Louis, *L'Assassinat de Coligny*. Geneva, Librairie Droz, 1992. ISBN 9782600039932.

Bourgeon, Jean-Louis, *Charles IX devant la Saint-Barthélemy*. Geneva, Librairie Droz, 1995. ISBN 9782600000901.

Browning, William Shergold, *The History of the Huguenots During the Sixteenth Century*. London, W Pickering, 1829.

Cornell, Paul, Martin Day and Keith Topping, *Doctor Who: The Discontinuity Guide*. London, Virgin Publishing, 1995. ISBN 9780426204428.

D'Aubigne, Jean-Henri Merle, *Histoire de la Reformation au XVIie Siècle*. Paris, Firmin Didot Frères, 1835.

Davis, Gerry and Alison Bingeman, *Doctor Who: The Celestial Toymaker*. **The Target Doctor Who Library** #111. London, W H Allen, 1987. ISBN 9780426202516.

Dicks, Terrance and Malcolm Hulke, *The Making of Doctor Who*. London, W H Allen, 1976. ISBN 9780426116158.

Dumas, Alexandre,, *Margaret of Navarre, Or the Massacre of Saint Bartholomew's Eve* (*La Reine Margot*). Unknown trans, London, G Pierce, 1846.

Dumas, Alexandre, *Marguerite de Valois: An Historical Romance* (*La Reine Margot*). Alexandrine-Sophie Goury de Champgrand, trans, London, David Bogue, 1846.

Dumas, Alexandre, *La Reine Margot*. David Coward, trans, Oxford, Oxford University Press, 1997. ISBN 9780192838445.

Faulkner, J Meade, *Moonfleet*. London, Edward Arnold, 1898.

Gilmont, Jean Francois, *John Calvin and the Printed Book*. Kirksville, Truman State University Press, 2005. ISBN 9781931112567.

Goethe, Johan Wolfgang, *Die Leiden des Jungen*. Leipzig, Weygand'sche Buchandlung, 1774.

Haag, Emile, and Eugene Haag, *The Protestant France*. Paris, Joel Cherbuliez, 1846-59.

Haining, Peter, *Doctor Who: A Celebration*. London, W H Allen, 1983. ISBN 9780491033510.

Holt, Mack P, *The French Wars of Religion, 1562–1629*. Cambridge, Cambridge University Press, 2005. ISBN 0521547504.

Horne, Alistair, *Seven Ages of Paris, Portrait of a City*. London, Pan, 2003. ISBN 9780330488648.

Howe, David J, and Stephen James Walker, *Doctor Who: The Television Companion*. London, BBC Books, 1998. ISBN 9780563405887.

Howe, David J, Mark Stammers and Stephen James Walker, *The Fourth Doctor*. **Doctor Who: The Handbook**. London, Virgin Publishing, 1992. ISBN 9780426203698.

Howe, David J, Mark Stammers and Stephen James Walker, *The Sixth Doctor*. **Doctor Who: The Handbook**. London, Virgin Publishing, 1993. ISBN 9780426204008.

Howe, David J, Mark Stammers and Stephen James Walker, *The First Doctor*. **Doctor Who: The Handbook**. London, Virgin Publishing, 1994. ISBN 9780426204301.

Howe, David J, Mark Stammers and Stephen James Walker, *The Third Doctor*. **Doctor Who: The Handbook**. London, Virgin Publishing, 1996. ISBN 9780426204862.

Howe, David J, Mark Stammers and Stephen James Walker, *The Second Doctor*. **Doctor Who: The Handbook**. London Publishing, Virgin, 1997. ISBN 9780426205166.

Howe, David J, Mark Stammers and Stephen James Walker, *The Fifth Doctor*. **Doctor Who: The Handbook**. London, Virgin Publishing, 1997. ISBN 9780426204589.

Howe, David J, Mark Stammers and Stephen James Walker, *The Seventh Doctor*. **Doctor Who: The Handbook**. London, Virgin Publishing, 1997. ISBN 9780426205272.

Kingdon, Robert McCune, *Geneva and the Consolidation of the French Protestant Movement, 1564-1572*. Madison, University of Wisconsin Press, 1967. ISBN 9780317559682.

Kingdon, Robert M, *Myths about the St Bartholomew's Day Massacres, 1572-1576*. Cambridge, Harvard University Press, 1988. ISBN 9780674182202.

Koenigsberger, H G, *Early Modern Europe 1500-1789*. Harlow, Longman, 1987. ISBN 058249401X.

Lawless Lee, Grace, *The Huguenot Settlements in Ireland*. London, Longmans Green, 1936.

Lucarotti, John, *Doctor Who: The Aztecs*. **The Target Doctor Who Library** #88. London, WH Allen, 1984. ISBN 978042619588.

Lucarotti, John, *Doctor Who: Marco Polo*. **The Target Doctor Who Library** #94. London, WH Allen, 1984. ISBN 9780426199670.

Lucarotti, John, *Doctor Who: The Massacre*. **The Target Doctor Who Library** #122. London, WH Allen, 1987. ISBN 9780491034234.

Marlowe, Christopher, ed Fredson Bowers, *The Complete Works of Christopher Marlowe Volume 1, Second Edition*. Cambridge, Cambridge University Press, 2009. ISBN 9780521090421.

Martène, Edmond, *Histoire de l'Abbaye de Marmoutier* vol 2. Tours, Guilland-Verger & Georget-Joubert , 1875.

Neale, J E, *The Age of Catherine de Medici*. London, Jonathan Cape, 1957.

Shearman, Robert, and Toby Hadoke, *Running Through Corridors, Rob and Toby's Marathon Watch of Doctor Who – Volume 1, The 60s*. Des Moines, Mad Norwegian Press, 2010. ISBN 978-1935234067.

Stevenson, Robert Louis, *Kidnapped*. London, Cassell & Co Ltd, 1886.

Sutherland, Nicola M, *The Massacre of Saint Bartholomew and the European Conflict, 1559-72*. London, Macmillan, 1973. ISBN 9780333136294.

Thorndike, Russell, *Doctor Syn: A Tale of the Romney Marsh*. Edinburgh, Thomas Nelson and Sons, 1915.

Whitehead, Barbara, 'Revising the Revisionists' in *Politics, Ideology and the Law in Early Modern Europe, Essays in Honor of J H M Salmon*. Rochester, University of Rochester Press, 1995. ISBN 9781878822390.

Wood, Tat, and Lawrence Miles, *1963-1966: Seasons 1 to 3*. **About Time: The Unauthorized Guide to Doctor Who**. Des Moines, Mad Norwegian Press, 2006. ISBN 9780975944608.

Periodicals

Doctor Who Magazine (DWM). Marvel UK, Panini, BBC, 1979-.

> Adams, Matt, 'Taking the Lead'. DWM #483, cover date March 2015.

> Hearn, Marcus, 'Script Editing Who, Donald Tosh'. DWM #191, cover date September 1992.

> Hearn, Marcus, 'Script Editing Who, Donald Tosh'. DWM #192, cover date October 1992.

> Lucarotti, John, 'Brief Encounter'. DWM #167, cover date 28 November 1990.

> Marson, Richard, 'Paddy's Field! Paddy Russell Interview'. DWM #127, cover date August 1987.

Pixley, Andrew, 'Archive: The Highlanders'. DWM #292, cover date June 2000.

Russell, Gary, 'Off The Shelf'. DWM #124, cover date May 1987.

'Sid The Rat', '25 Five Years Of Turkeys'. DWM #144, cover date January 1989.

Smith, Paul J, 'The Season Survey Results'. DWM #150, cover date July 1989.

Stephens, Adam, and Matthew Brooke, 'The Show Must Go On'. DWM #487, cover date May 2015.

TARDIS:

McLachlan, Ian, 'The John Wiles Interview Part 1', *TARDIS* vol 6 #1, 1981.

McLachlan, Ian, 'The John Wiles Interview Part 2', *TARDIS* vol 6 #2, 1981.

Bentham, J Jeremy, 'John Wiles Interview'. *Doctor Who Winter Special*, 1983.

Nelson, Eric, 'The Legacy of Iconoclasm, Religious war and the relic landscape of Tours, Blois and Vendôme, 1550-1750'. *St Andrews Studies in French History and Culture* #6. St Andrews, Centre for French History and Culture, September 2013.

Radio Times, 5 to 13 February 1966, published Thursday 3 February 1966.

Tweed, Robert, 'The Massacre'. *DreamWatch Bulletin* #117, cover date September 1993

Television

Doctor Who. BBC, 1963-.

Elizabeth R. BBC, 1971.

'Shadow in the Sun' (episode 3).

Film

Davies, Kevin, dir, *Dalekmania*. Lumiere Films, 1993.

Davies, Kevin, dir, *Doctor Who: More Than 30 Years In The TARDIS*. BBC, 1995.

Dréville, Jean, dir, *La Reine Margot*. Lux Compagnie Cinématographique de France, 1954.

Griffith, D W, dir, *Intolerance: Love's Struggle Throughout the Ages*. Triangle Film Corporation, 1916.

Hooper, Tom, dir, *Les Misérables*. Working Title Films, 2012.

LeRoy, Mervyn, dir, *Quo Vadis*. MGM, 1951.

Sturges, John, dir, *Gunfight at the OK Corral*. Paramount Pictures, 1957.

Websites

'Doctor Who: The Classic Series – The Massacre'. BBC online. http://www.bbc.co.uk/doctorwho/classic/episodeguide/massacre/detail.shtml. Accessed 4 December 2015.

'Minutes. 1572, Janvier – 1572, 27 Août'. Archives Nationales.
https://www.siv.archives-
nationales.culture.gouv.fr/siv/rechercheconsultation/consultation/i
r/consultationIR.action?udId=c1p6sfinjpqr-
e9bobsuzq003&consIr=&irId=FRAN_IR_041146&frontIr=&auSeinIR
=true. Accessed 4 December 2015.

St Augustine, *Tractates on the Gospel of John*. John Gibb, trans,
New Advent. http://www.newadvent.org/fathers/1701.htm.
Accessed 4 December 2015.

Pixley, Andrew, 'By Any Other Name'. The New Zealand Doctor
Who Fan Club, December 2007.
http://doctorwho.org.nz/archive/tsv54/byanyothername.html.
Accessed 4 December 2015.

Sandifer, Philip, 'Not always. I'm Sorry. (The Massacre)'.
Eruditorium Press, April 2011.
http://www.philipsandifer.com/blog/not-always-im-sorry-the-
massacre/. Accessed 4 December 2015.

Smith, Kenny, 'Doctor Who story editor Donald Tosh on his
contribution to the Time Lord's series in 1965-66'. *Scotland Now*,
11 September 2004.
http://www.scotlandnow.dailyrecord.co.uk/lifestyle/doctor-who-
story-editor-donald-4282399. Accessed 4 December 2015.

Stevens, Alan, 'Donald Tosh Interview'. Kaldor City.
www.kaldorcity.com/people/dtinterview.html. Accessed 4
December 2015.

BIOGRAPHY

James Cooray Smith has written for *The New Statesman*, *Private Eye* and **That Mitchell and Webb Sound**, and is the author of about a dozen books of film and television criticism, almost none of which are still in print. He contributed the Production Information Subtitles to several official BBC **Doctor Who** DVD releases, and has written audio adventures for both **Professor Bernice Summerfield** and *The Robots of Death* spin-off series **Kaldor City,** as well as a prose novella featuring Professor Challenger and Iris Wildthyme for Obverse Books. He lives in North London with a Lady Barrister.